HEAVEN'S TRUTH

The Parallels Between the Bible and
the Near-Death Experience

Jay W. Spillers

Copyright © 2020 Jay W. Spillers

All rights reserved

The characters and events portrayed in this book are fictitious. Any similarity to real persons, living or dead, is coincidental and not intended by the author.

No part of this book may be reproduced, or stored in a retrieval system, or transmitted in any form or by any means, electronic, mechanical, photocopying, recording, or otherwise, without express written permission of the publisher.

ISBN: 9798666106006

Cover design by: Art Painter
Library of Congress Control Number: 2018675309
Printed in the United States of America

CONTENTS

Title Page
Copyright
DEDICATION — 1
PREFACE — 2
INTRODUCTION — 5
1. THE MIRROR — 8
2. NDE-LIKE EXPERIENCES — 17
3. JESUS — 30
4. SPIRITUAL REALMS — 41
5. LOVE — 52
6. LIGHT — 59
7. JUDGMENT — 65
8. SALVATION — 73
9. OBJECTION! — 84
10. SCHOOL — 91
11. EVIDENCE — 98
CONCLUSION — 114
ABOUT THE AUTHOR — 116

DEDICATION

To my loving wife Linda and our son Timothy and to my parents Harold and Linda who have crossed over to heaven.

PREFACE

I first came to Christ at the age of 9 at a summer day camp for the blind and visually impaired in Southern California. I was born with a visual impairment that I've had my entire life. An older camper was sharing Jesus with me and invited me to receive Christ as my Lord and Savior which I did. I was so nervous but knew from that point on, my life was different, there was no question in my mind. Though I didn't always follow Jesus as I knew I should, I knew that Jesus had come into my heart and things would never be the same. Looking back, I can see how God kept bringing me back to himself and guiding my life.

I quickly started attending a church soon after I came to Christ with my older sister Janet who had recently moved back home. I attended a well-known mega-church, Calvary Chapel, Costa Mesa which had been started and led by Chuck Smith in the 1960's. Chuck Smith was one of the leaders in the Jesus Movement which led many hippies to Christ in the late 60's and early 70's. His church became the flagship church for the Calvary Chapel movement. He led and mentored other pastors in the movement which went on to become popular in their own right such as Greg Lourie who today has become the next Billy Graham. When I started attending the church in the early 1980s, it still had a hippy vibe to it. I thoroughly enjoyed Calvary Chapel and would spend hours listening to sermons by various pastors on tape with Janet in addition to attending services throughout the week.

A couple years later, at the age of 11, I remember watching a TV show called "That's Incredible" which was a popular show in the early 80s that covered amazing stories. On one program they were covering near-death experiences (NDE). I was absolutely fascinated. Here were people today who had actually gone to heaven and met God or Jesus in person. This was covering what I believed by faith with a first-hand account of the other side.

I was so impressed by the show that I thought I would call a popular Christian radio program that sought to answer questions about matters of faith. The show was called "The Bible Answerman" and was hosted by Dr. Walter Martin. He was well-known for his work on the "cults" and Christian apologetics which deals with defending the Christian faith and giving reasons for it. I was able to get on the program which I was recording on cassette with a tape recorder up against the radio. I told Dr. Martin about the show and asked what he thought. The answer was a bit of a let down, to say the least. His response was extremely dismissive, to the point of practically dismissing the young caller. I felt like he was basically saying "kid, you're asking nonsense". This was back in 1983, you can do the math on my age. At the time and for many years thereafter, the Christian world was largely closed to the idea of the NDE.

For the most part, I put the issue aside for several years, but would occasionally have my interest briefly resparked if I caught a special on TV about the NDE. It wasn't until 1997 in my third year in law school that I really became re-interested in the topic. I had started to have doubts in my faith and found some doctrines such as hell to be troubling. Over the next 20 years I dived into the study more thoroughly.

From my memory, I have read over a dozen books on the topic of the near-death experience. Most were personal testimonies, many of which were from Christians who have had an NDE. I have also read some research books. Most of my education about the NDE, however, has come from reading and hearing literally hundreds if not thousands of near-death experiences online, in movies, and on TV. I've spent countless hours researching the NDE online. I have belonged to numerous list groups, Facebook groups, and message boards over the years.

In terms of my Christian faith, it has gone full circle partly due to my study of the NDE. I don't have any doubts, and my faith is stronger than it's ever been. The NDE has taken my faith to much deeper levels of understanding. The near-death experience has been the ultimate apologetic for my faith. With reading and hearing many NDEs, it always struck me how much it parallels the Bible and the Christian faith in virtually every respect. It might contradict some interpretations of scripture, but as far as I could see, never contradicted the Word. In fact, it affirmed the validity of the Bible. It amazes me that more books have not been written about the common message that both teach. I believe it has a common truth because both come from the same source which is God.

Over the past few years, there has started to be more openness to the NDE in Christian circles which is fantastic. Many books and movies have been released and more are set to come down the pipeline. Many influential Christian leaders, including some within the world of Apologetics, have come around to it since Dr. Martin's time. At least 3 apologists come to mind which include Frank Turek, William Lane Craig, and Gary Habermas. Dr. Habermas has actually gone further and is now studying the near-death experience to gain expertise in them. He already is known for his work on the Resurrection within the field of apologetics. As far as I can see, Habermas is treating the NDE as another avenue for apologetics of the Faith.

If you would like to contact me after reading this book, you may email me at spillers72@gmail.com. You may also follow spiritual discussions further on Facebook at https://www.facebook.com/Spiritual-Discussion-Page-106913824248676/?modal=admin_todo_tour

INTRODUCTION

The near-death experience (NDE) gives a vivid and compelling illustration of some of what we read in the scriptures. It brings our faith to life in an exceedingly profound way. You don't have to have had an NDE yourself to appreciate what the phenomena can give you. Just reading or hearing the accounts can confirm the reality of scripture to you. We read about powerful spiritual experiences in the Bible, and they, of course, do bring us hope, but some of it at times can seem so far removed from us due to the lapse of time between us in the 21st century and them thousands of years ago. It can make your heart leap for joy knowing that a place called heaven is real and that people alive today have been there. You could actually meet and talk to these people who have had near-death experiences.

What will become abundantly clear as one reads through this book is that virtually everything learned or experienced in a near-death experience (NDE) correlates to what the Bible teaches in one way or another. This is when the NDE is analyzed on the whole and not just a single near-death experience. You can always find an outlining NDE that doesn't seem to fit with the scriptures, but when you look at NDEs collectively, you begin to see clear patterns. You have to seek to gain a context for the experience as a whole. This is really much the same with the scriptures, any good Bible teacher would tell you never to take one verse or portion of scripture in isolation but to study the scriptures as a whole.

One of the main questions in the New Testament is who is Jesus? As Peter rightly declared "You are the Christ, the Son of the living God." (Mathew 16:16). This question of who Jesus is doesn't come up in every near-death experience, but when it has, the basic truth that Jesus is the Son of God is always confirmed. I've literally never seen a near-death experience where someone was told that Jesus was in fact, not the Son of God. There are also NDEs that have confirmed other facts about Jesus such as his taking away sins on the cross or that he will come again someday.

The Bible clearly teaches that it's inspired by God and worthy of teaching and guiding people in their daily lives (II Timothy 3:16). In every instance where the question of the Bible has come up in a near-death experience, this basic truth has been affirmed. Again, in no NDE that I've ever seen or heard, has the Bible's divine inspiration ever been denied. This is key because if the NDE can be supported by evidence as a genuine spiritual experience, it would indirectly affirm the scriptures. The same is also true, that if the Bible effectively affirms the validity of the NDE and it can be supported by evidence, that would indirectly affirm the validity of the NDE. Not all claims of an NDE necessarily but the experience in general.

The Bible teaches clearly that God is Light and this is how many in scripture experienced God in direct encounters. This is exactly one of the main features of the near-death experience is to encounter a being of Light that is all-encompassing. The scriptures also teach the centrality of love in terms of living your life for God. This is especially true within the New Testament. Anyone that has even briefly looked at the near-death experience would know that love is without question, the main feature of the experience. Love is everything literally. God is love and this is the main purpose for life is to love. Love actually holds things together. You could say, love does make the world go round. All of the sappy songs about how we need more love are actually spot on in that respect to truth from the NDE.

The near-death experience supports the biblical notion of an afterlife which includes the concepts of heaven and hell. This also includes the idea of a Judgment to come after we die, where we give an accounting of our life before God.

My hope with this book is that it will affirm a believers' faith in Christ as well as to offer additional hope. This book may also give hope to those that are not yet believers and help them to believe that there is a God that genuinely loves and cares for them. The near-death experience has become the most powerful apologetic for my faith and my trust in the scriptures.

I think many will find this book helpful in comparing the scriptures with the near-death experience whether or not you are a Christian and regardless of what background you happen to come from. This book may help to bridge the gap between the Christian community and the NDE community which sometimes overlaps but sometimes not.

All scripture references unless otherwise noted are from the New King James Version.

1. THE MIRROR

The Bible and the near-death experience are like a mirror in that they reflect back to each other. The Bible points to the near-death experience and what I call NDE-like experiences throughout scripture. We will discuss a few key ones. The near-death experience has also affirmed the Bible when the subject has been broached or brought up in the experience. Sometimes in profound ways.

The first area to start in is seeing if there are actually any direct near-death experiences within the scriptures. There are arguably only two NDEs in scripture, but they're central to the Christian faith and the Bible itself. The first one is a near-death experience that the Apostle Paul had. The next one is the Resurrection of Jesus.

Finally, we will look at two cases where the Bible was powerfully affirmed by near-death experiences.

Near-Death Experiences in the Bible

The NDE of the Apostle Paul

The scriptures never uses the phrase near-death experience, so Paul isn't going to be referring to his near-death experience. The term was first coined in 1975 by Ramond Moody in his groundbreaking book "Life After Life". NDEs have occurred throughout history but became more commonly reported starting in the 1970s due to improved resuscitation techniques.

Paul records what I believe to be his near-death experience in II Corinthians 12:2-4:

[2] I know a man in Christ who fourteen years ago—whether in the body I do not

know, or whether out of the body I do not know, God knows—such a one was caught up to the third heaven. [3] And I know such a man—whether in the body or out of the body I do not know, God knows— [4] how he was caught up into Paradise and heard inexpressible words, which it is not lawful for a man to utter.

If this is a near-death experience, when did Paul die and come back to life? Paul probably died when he was stoned by the Jews for preaching the gospel at Lystra in Acts 12:19 which says "[19] Then Jews from Antioch and Iconium came there; and having persuaded the multitudes, they stoned Paul *and* dragged *him* out of the city, supposing him to be dead."

Notice in the passage above that they thought he was dead and were able to drag what appeared to be his lifeless body completely out of the city. He was either dead or close to death. Clearly, he was not conscious. In the next verse, he had regained consciousness as it said "[20] However, when the disciples gathered around him, he rose up and went into the city. And the next day he departed with Barnabas to Derbe." This entire experience is enough to have easily triggered a near-death experience.

Breaking down the passage in II Corinthians 12:2-4, we start with " I know a man in Christ who fourteen years ago". Scholars generally would take this to be Paul referring to himself. He goes on to say "whether in the body I do not know, or whether out of the body I do not know, God knows". Paul seems unclear about what state he was in physically. He repeats the phrase whether in the body or out of the body, so it was something unfamiliar to him at the time. The event seems to be more than just a vision because he tells us that the man was taken to the third heaven and paradise, not that he just glimpsed it.

Possibly, like other NDEers, he was given a spirit body that felt like a real body but differed from that of the physical one in certain ways. Paul even taught about how we would eventually be given a spiritual body in I Corinthians 15:44 "It is sown a natural body, it is raised a spiritual body. There is a natural body, and there is a spiritual body." Paul may have been recounting the story from the man as he would have understood it when the event occurred in Acts, later, Paul was given revelation from God concerning our spiritual bodies.

Paul then goes on to say "such a one was caught up to the third heaven". There are three levels of heaven taught in scripture, the first heaven is what we would call the sky. The second heaven is space. The third heaven is where God resides, it's the realm of great peace, joy, and love. This is what most of us think of when we speak of heaven. He then tells us he was caught up into paradise.

Paradise simply means garden. Many near-death experiencers mention being in a garden when they first enter heaven. Some don't go beyond that point, some go further. Within this garden, people can have encounters with God, Jesus, angels, and departed loved ones. Paradise functions like an entryway into heaven. Possibly before Christ came, believers were only able to enter paradise but could not ascend further into heaven. They waited in what was called "Abraham's bosom".

Jesus told the thief on the cross in Luke 23:43 "today, you will be with me in Paradise". This is the corridor leading to heaven. Why would Paul only be permitted to enter paradise but go no further? The answer is probably that his work was not done, and he would be going back to complete it. We know from his ministry and the scripture he wrote, he had a lot more work to do. Some NDEers are given a choice to come back, and some are simply told it's not their time and that they have to come back. My guess is, Paul was not given a choice.

The verses say that he was "caught up" into heaven and paradise, which implies to me that he was transported rather than just instantaneously appearing there. This may be why he mentions going to the third heaven. He was caught up or flying through the sky and space toward paradise. Many near-death experiencers experience being transported through the air and space before reaching heaven.

Paul makes it clear in II Corinthians 5:8 "We are confident, yes, well pleased rather to be absent from the body and to be present with the Lord." We may not immediately be in heaven upon death, but the Lord is present with us as we ascend up. Many NDEers have reported feeling a presence of love and warmth even before they see the Light and start to move toward heaven. God will be with us every step of the way when it's our time to pass on.

The passage concludes with what he experienced in paradise, he "heard inexpressible words, which it is not lawful for a man to utter". This passage is quoted from the New King James Version. The King James uses the phrase "unspeakable words" for inexpressible words. The Greek word for unspeakable is arrētos (Strong's Concordance G731) which refers to unspoken words due to the beauty and sacredness.[1] In the Young's Literal Translation which is one of the most literal translations into English, it says "heard unutterable sayings".

So, if the words were unspoken or not uttered, how were they transmitted to Paul? The answer is probably that they were communicated telepathically. Virtually every near-death experiencer has said that words spoken to them on the other side were not spoken with the mouth but telepathically or something akin to it. The words would simply be put within their mind at amazing speeds. Sometimes a question would be answered before the person could complete the question. Because communication is mind to mind without spoken words, speaking a different language is not an issue. A person that dies in America today that speaks only English could easily communicate with Paul who spoke Hebrew and Greek if they were to encounter him on the other side.

When speaking of what he saw and heard, he then says "which it is not lawful for a man to utter." This may cause a bit of confusion for the reader in English. The word for lawful in Greek is *exesti* (Strong's (G1832) which can mean lawful or permitted but can also simply mean possible.) Young's translates it "that it is not possible for man to speak" in verse 4. Paul was not prohibited from speaking about his experience, he just did to some extent. He was not able in words to fully express what he experienced. Many NDEers have expressed frustration in trying to put into words what they experienced on the other side, it's just too beautiful and fantastic.

So why is Paul's NDE so important? Considering the fact that he wrote 13 books of the Bible and possibly 14 if he wrote Hebrews, it's not hard to understand. He wrote roughly half of the New Testament. Paul himself was one of the most influential Apostles in the New Testament and brought the faith to the gentiles or nations. This experience no doubt helped to transform his life and spiritual walk with God. It invariably influenced his entire teaching and ministry including what he gave us in scripture.

His experience recorded in scripture is a profound testimony of the reality of the NDE for us today. It helps to bridge the world of the Bible with what we see in our world with near-death experiences today. One thing you see in the writings of Paul more clearly than any other New Testament writer is that he had absolutely no fear of death.

He said in Philippians 1:21 "For to me, to live *is* Christ, and to die *is* gain." He actually says death is something to be gained, it's better than this life. Notice, he personalizes it by saying "for to me". He's speaking from his heart out of personal experience.

He teaches in I Cor 15:54 concerning death "[54] So when this corruptible has put on incorruption, and this mortal has put on immortality, then shall be brought to pass the saying that is written: "Death is swallowed up in victory." We have victory over death. He goes on in that same chapter to teach that death and the grave has no sting because we have victory in Jesus. (See verses

55-57)

Paul teaches that in this world we have limited knowledge and understanding but in heaven, we shall have a more full understanding. We will get the bigger picture as to why we are here and what it all means. As he says in I Corinthians 13:12 "For now we see in a mirror, dimly, but then face to face. Now I know in part, but then I shall know just as I also am known." This passage is just a chapter over from where he recounts his near-death experience.

The Resurrection of Jesus as an NDE

The Resurrection of Jesus is on a much grander scale than a typical near-death experience. I would still classify it as an NDE because Christ died and was fully conscious while physically dead and finally came back to life. His near-death experience was a highly extraordinary one, to say the least.

Jesus knew that he would die and come back to life three days later (Mathew 20:17-19), but he also knew that he would be active and fully aware on the other side while his body was in the grave. He told the thief on the cross "today, you will be with me in Paradise" (Luke 23:43). He also told his disciples leading up to his death that he was going to prepare a place for them in heaven in John 14:1-4

> Let not your heart be troubled; you believe in God, believe also in Me. ² In My Father's house are many [a]mansions; if *it were* not *so,* [b]I would have told you. I go to prepare a place for you. ³ And if I go and prepare a place for you, I will come again and receive you to Myself; that where I am, *there* you may be also. ⁴ And where I go you know, and the way you know.

The scriptures also record that Jesus was at work in the spiritual realms while in the grave. Jesus had to first descend into hell or hades and bring souls up to heaven. Many, no doubt were believers who were in Abraham's bosom, but some were actually in hell and were sinners in judgment. We can clearly see this in I Peter 3:18-20:

> ¹⁸ For Christ also suffered once for sins, the just for the unjust, that He might bring [f]us to God, being put to death in the flesh but made alive by the

Spirit, [19] by whom also He went and preached to the spirits in prison, [20] who formerly were disobedient, [g]when once the Divine longsuffering waited in the days of Noah, while *the* ark was being prepared, in which a few, that is, eight souls, were saved through water.

Notice, the passage says the spirits were in prison and that they had been disobedient. It goes on to say that their disobedience happened in the days of Noah when only eight people survived. These are not demons but actual humans. I'm sure there were other souls who were preached to in hades and ascended up with Christ as well, but the ones in Noah's day are specifically mentioned. Probably everyone that perished before the coming of Christ had an opportunity to receive the gospel directly from Jesus..

In the next chapter, Peter goes on with this teaching and says "For this reason the gospel was preached also to those who are dead, that they might be judged according to men in the flesh, but live according to God in the spirit." (I Peter 4:6). It would seem clear that all those that had died physically and fell into judgment were given a chance to hear the good news. The people may have been given a special dispensation of grace to hear the gospel because they came before Christ and had no knowledge of Christ. This is true even though they had been dead possibly for thousands of years.

Paul talked about the same thing as Peter when he wrote in Ephesians 4:8-10:

[8] Therefore He says:

"When He ascended on high,
He led captivity captive,
And gave gifts to men.
[9] (Now this, "He ascended"—what does it mean but that He also [d]first descended into the lower parts of the earth? [10] He who descended is also the One who ascended far above all the heavens, that He might fill all things.)

Jesus had to first descend into hades to gather both the righteous and the unrighteous who chose to believe the gospel into heaven. We know that he achieved this portion within the first day because he told the thief it would be today that he would be with him in paradise. The other two days were spent all in heaven. While in heaven, Jesus was preparing places for his disciples as well as other believers who would come when they pass from their life on earth. He was also busy giving gifts to those who entered into the heavenly realms.

Jesus ascended above the heavens which is when the other levels of heaven besides paradise would be opened to believers.

Why is this extraordinary near-death experience of Jesus, the Resurrection, so critical? The Resurrection is the heart of the Christian faith, as Paul says in I Corinthians 15:14 "if Christ is not risen, then our preaching *is* empty and your faith *is* also empty." The resurrection is the central event in human history. If it is an NDE, it gives profound credence to the near-death experience in general. Jesus gave hope not only to himself between his death and resurrection but to millions of people he preached to. The NDE is giving hope to millions today that there is truly life after death and a God that loves them.

The Bible in Near-Death Experiences

The Testimony of Emmanuel Tuwagirairmana

Emmanuel was a Tutsi minority living in Rwanda during the war in 1994. He was injured in his left arm and had to seek refuge with a number of other Tutsis in a school. His wounds grew worse and he was eventually found dead by some of his companions. They wrapped him in bed sheets but could not bury him because it was too dangerous to leave the school.

When Emmanuel died, he left his body and found himself at a gate. Emmanuel was a Christian at the time of his death. An angel greeted him and brought him to the entrance to heaven. He then met Jesus. Christ first showed him the wounds in his hands and then he saw Christ in perfection. Jesus began to give him a tour of heaven.

Emmanuel saw a huge lake with a bright light on the other

side. He was told that God's throne was on the other side and that he could not go there now because it was not his time. Emmanuel was given what looked like a tablet of chocolate and told to eat it. He ate it and was told by Jesus that he had consumed the entire Bible. He would know it word for word from that point forward when he returned.

When Emmanuel did return to earth, he did know the entire Bible which has been testified to by others. This is a testament to the power and importance of the Bible that came out of an NDE. It's also a miraculous impartation of scripture as a result of his near-death experience.[2]

Howard Storms question about the Bible during his NDE

Howard Storm was an atheist before his near-death experience, but became a Christian and a pastor after he met Jesus on the other side. His story is more fully told in the Chapter entitled "Jesus". Howard was rescued from hell by Jesus and was able to ask Jesus a number of questions on a variety of topics. The question of the Bible came up, and he asked Jesus about the Bible. Howard wanted to know if it was truly inspired or not. He had tried to read the Bible a few times but found it difficult to understand. He was told that it was inspired and that it was spiritually true. You do have to read it prayerfully and spiritually to gain its truths on a deeper level. Others have also been able to ask directly whether the scriptures are divinely inspired or not and have always been told that they are inspired by God. This confirms what II Timothy 3:16 says "All scripture is given by inspiration of God, and is profitable for doctrine, for reproof, for correction, for instruction in righteousness:" (KJV)

Howard's testimony of the scriptures is a good one to add to Emmanuels because, unlike Emmanuel, he was not a Christian before his NDE, he was an atheist and obviously did not believe in the Bible before his experience. Both give powerful testimony to the scriptures in their own unique way.[3]

2. NDE-LIKE EXPERIENCES

What we find more often in the Bible than near-death experiences is what I call NDE-like experiences which resemble a near-death experience but don't involve people actually dying. In most cases, the person isn't even close to death. They're usually fully alive while having the experience. One case where the person was on the verge of dying but probably couldn't be classified as an NDE in a strict sense was Stephen in the book of Acts. He clearly had a vision just before dying but didn't come back to life. He also had not left his body while having his experience. This would be classified as a deathbed vision.

These types of NDE-like experiences in the near-death experience world are called spiritually transformative experiences (STE). Many people who have an interest in the NDE usually also study STEs alongside the near-death experience. It's not uncommon for people who have had an NDE to also have STEs. Sometimes prior to having an NDE or following an NDE. It may be that one experience can later help to trigger the other. I believe the Apostle Paul had an STE on the road to Damascus which led to his conversion and calling to ministry. He later would have a near-death experience after being stoned years later.

Moses Directly Encounters God

God appeared to Moses while he was tending his father-law Jetho's Sheep he came to Mt. Horeb as it says in Exodus 3:2-6

> And the Angel of the Lord appeared to him in a flame of fire from the midst of a bush. So he looked, and behold, the bush was burning with fire,

but the bush *was* not consumed. 3 Then Moses said, "I will now turn aside and see this great sight, why the bush does not burn."

4 So when the Lord saw that he turned aside to look, God called to him from the midst of the bush and said, "Moses, Moses!"

And he said, "Here I am."

5 Then He said, "Do not draw near this place. Take your sandals off your feet, for the place where you stand *is* holy ground." 6 Moreover He said, "I *am* the God of your father—the God of Abraham, the God of Isaac, and the God of Jacob." And Moses hid his face, for he was afraid to look upon God.

Dov Steinmetz, in his article "Revelation" on Mount Horeb as a Near-Death Experience" points out three similarities between this experience and the NDE that are of interest and make it an NDE-like experience.

The first one is that Moses saw the flame of fire that was in the midst of the bush. This light was comparable to that of what NDEers see. Sometimes it's described as a light or what appears to be like a fire. Did Moses see a literal fire or a light that shimmered and pulsated? It's difficult to say, such a light would appear to be like a flame to him. The light that he saw didn't consume the bush which Moses found astounding.

This experience with God transformed Moses and would forever change the direction of his life. He went from being a shepherd of his father-laws sheep to a prophet, law-giver, and the one to lead his people out of bondage into the promised land. This was going to be his purpose from the beginning and now God was calling him to it.

Moses had a sense of mission that guided him the rest of his life that started with Horeb. Many near-death experiencers go through the same experience of seeing the light, being transformed, and being given a sense of mission when they go back to earth. Often, they're specifically told what their mission is to be when they come back. It may be simply to share love, hope, or a more specific message from God for people to hear.[4]

I would add a fourth aspect to what Moses experienced after his first encounter with God, which are miracles that followed his calling. This would include the ten plagues; the parting of the Red Sea; being led by God through a cloud; and manna from heaven. Some NDEers have had their experience followed by miracles when they returned as well.

Moses' experiences would culminate in an even more direct experience with God in Exodus 33:18-34:35. Moses had asked to see God's glory. God agreed and said specifically in 33:22,23 "22 So it shall be, while My glory passes by, that I will put you in the cleft of the rock, and will cover you with My hand while I pass by. 23 Then I will take away My hand, and you shall see My back; but My face shall not be seen."

Apparently, Moses had seen some of God's awesomeness at Horeb but not His full glory. Moses was given a more direct view of God now, but it was still limited. He was only able to see the back of God. What does this mean exactly? Does God literally have a face and backside? Probably not, this was a way for God to express to Moses what he was experiencing that would make sense to him and his readers. Its allegorical language.

Not being able to see the totality of God is not surprising, even NDEers don't necessarily see all that God is in the Light. Pam Reynolds asked if the Light was God during her near-death experience and was told that it was the Breath of God.[5] What's interesting is that the Holy Spirit is understood to be the breath of God. The Spirit is a personal being, of course, but still the Breath of God. So the Light is the Holy Spirit. The Holy Spirit is also the same as the Spirit of Christ (Romans 8:9). It would thus be correct to say that the Light or being of Light is Christ even if the experiencer doesn't see the human form of Jesus during the experience.

The Mount of Transfiguration

The story of the Mount of Transfiguration is told in several passages of scripture. (Mathew 17:1-8, Mark 9:2-8, Luke 9:28-36, and II Peter 1:16-18). Jesus took Peter, James, and John unto a high Mountain and was glorified before them with a magnificent brightness to him. Jesus was joined by Moses and Elijah who came from heaven to meet with him. The Disciples present were awestruck by it all, and Peter requested to build an altar to Jesus, Moses, and Elijah. God the Father then enveloped them in a cloud and told them that Jesus was his Son and to listen to him. Peter witnessed many miracles of Christ, yet in II Peter:16-18, he uses the Mount of Transfiguration to establish the truth of his testimony, an event that resembles the Near-Death Experience.

> For we did not follow cunningly devised fables when we made known to you the power and coming of our Lord Jesus Christ, but were eyewitnesses of His majesty. [17] For He received from God the Father honor and glory when such a voice came to Him from the Excellent Glory: "This is My beloved Son, in whom I am well pleased." [18] And we heard this voice which came from heaven when we were with Him on the holy mountain.

Jesus Shines Brighter Than The Sun

Jesus began to shine with a dazzling light as Mathew 17:2 says, "and He was transfigured before them. His face shone like the sun, and His clothes became as white as the light." Many have seen Jesus appearing to shine with a brightness all around him from every direction during their NDE. They describe a light brighter than anything they have seen on earth. Sometimes they know it's Jesus specifically, sometimes it's just a being of Light with an indiscernible face. Jesus can sometimes appear normally and take on a brightness as he did in these verses.

Jesus appears to John again in a similar glorified appearance in Revelations 1:14-16 which says,

> 13 and in the midst of the seven lampstands *One* like the Son of Man, clothed with a garment down to the feet and girded about the chest with a golden band. 14 His head and hair *were* white like wool, as white as snow, and His eyes like a flame of fire; 15 His feet *were* like fine brass, as if refined in a furnace, and His voice as the sound of many waters; 16 He had in His right hand seven stars, out of His mouth went a sharp two-edged sword, and His countenance *was* like the sun shining in its strength.

The Appearance of Moses and Elijah

Moses and Elijah appeared to Jesus because they represent the law and the prophets which Jesus was to fulfill with his coming. Moses representing the law and Elijah, the prophets. In Luke 9:30, 31 it says "And behold, two men talked with Him, who were Moses and Elijah, [31] who appeared in glory and spoke of His [c]decease which He was about to accomplish at Jerusalem." This alludes to the fact that Jesus would be fulfilling the law and prophets with his crucifixion.

What's intriguing is that Peter knew that the two men were Moses and Elijah, though they lived centuries before him. Mathew 17:4 says "Then Peter answered and said to Jesus, "Lord, it is good for us to be here; if You wish, [a]let us make here three tabernacles: one for You, one for Moses, and one for Elijah" It's possible that Jesus could have told Peter, James, and John who they were, but nothing in the passage indicates that he did. It seems to be more of an intuitive knowing on Peter's part. It's not uncommon for people in NDEs to intuitively know who people are such as ancestors they never met or religious figures. No introduction is needed in the spiritual realm such as an NDE, or in this case, the Mount of Transfiguration.

Jesus and the Father are Present Together

We know that God the Father was present with Jesus because he speaks from heaven and surrounds the Disciples in a cloud. Mathew 17:5 says "While he was still speaking, behold, a bright cloud overshadowed them; and suddenly a voice came out of the cloud, saying, "This is My beloved Son, in whom I am well pleased. Hear Him!" In some NDEs such as that of Betty Eadie, both the Father and the Son have been known to be present with the individual.[6] The NDE thus gives indirect evidence for the Trinity. The two are one yet distinct.

Stephen Sees a Vision of Heaven before His Death

Stephen was able to receive a vision of heaven before he was martyred for his faith. (Acts 7:54-60). This was just after he had preached a message about Christ and how His people had killed the Messiah of God. He looked up to heaven and saw God and Christ in heaven on the throne. Stephan at the point of his vision was perfectly well and had not been stoned yet. Sometimes people will receive visions of the other side or have Jesus or a loved one visit them when they're about to die. They can be well and about to die in some manner, or have an illness where their death is approaching. Deathbed visions are like Near-Death Experiences in that the person sees heaven or is visited by someone from the other side, but they're not dead yet as is the case with the NDE. The event can give a great deal of peace and comfort and be a transformative experience.

Stephan Sees Christ at the Right Hand of God

Acts 7:55, 56 says "But he, being full of the Holy Spirit, gazed into heaven and saw the glory of God, and Jesus standing at the right hand of God, [56] and said, "Look! I see the heavens opened and the Son of Man standing at the right hand of God!" Notice that Stephan was full of the Holy Spirit. He was a Godly man and full of the Spirit in a general sense, but in this event, one has to believe that he was being held by the Spirit. The Spirit was there to offer a glimpse of heaven to give him greater peace in these final moments of Stephen's life.

In the verse above, Stephan like the Disciples on the Mount of Transfiguration saw Jesus and God the Father together. It says God, but usually, when God is mentioned in addition to Christ, it's referring to the Father. Stephen was experiencing the entire Trinity at this time, being filled with the Holy Spirit and seeing Jesus and the Father.

The Crowd's response to Stephen's Vision

From the next verses in 57, 58, the crowd didn't appear to see what Stephan saw and were enraged by his testimony of it as it says "Then they cried out with a loud voice, stopped their ears, and ran at him with one accord; [58] and they cast *him* out of the city and stoned *him*. And the witnesses laid down their clothes at the feet of a young man named Saul. In verse 59, they stone him "And they stoned Stephen as he was calling on *God* and saying, "Lord Jesus, receive my spirit." In these verses, we are introduced to Saul who would become Paul. Paul would go on to have his own NDE-like experience as well as an actual NDE. Stephen may have planted the seed for Paul's own conversion at this point. Paul's experiences were further confirmed to him as he remembered back to what Stephen had testified to.

Stephen's Heart was Further Transformed prior to His Death

Stephan was known from the first mention of him in scripture to be a Godly man in Acts 6:5 it says " And the saying pleased the whole multitude. And they chose Stephen, a man full of faith and the Holy Spirit". This was when Stephan was chosen as a Deacon. So, the vision he had in the next chapter was not of a man that did a 180-degree turn. I do have to think that he was further expanded in his spiritual walk through this vision. In Acts 7:60 it says " Then he knelt down and cried out with a loud voice, "Lord, do not charge them with this sin." And when he had said this, he fell asleep." He was able to follow in what Christ said when he died in Luke 23:34 "Then Jesus said, "Father, forgive them, for they do not know what they do." Stephan was able to give the people one last testimony of Christ from a profound heart of love. Could Stephan have been able to say this without the vision? Possibly, but it would seem that the vision gave him the added strength.

Paul's Conversion on the Road to Damascus

Paul had started out as a Pharisee and fierce persecutor of the church as we saw with Stephen. Paul, who was Saul at this time, was sent to round up and arrest any Christians he discovered on his journey to Damascus. On the road, Jesus appeared to him in a bright light and confronted him. Saul fell to the ground and asked who he was, and was told that it was Jesus who he had been persecuting. At this point, Paul was told that he would be a witness to all men and that he would receive further instructions within the city. The men who accompanied Paul partially experienced what Paul did but were unable to see Jesus specifically or hear him speaking. The account of Paul's encounter with Christ is in Acts 9:3-19, Acts 22:9-16, and Acts 26:19-26.

Paul's encounter with the risen Christ was the basis that Paul used to establish his Apostleship. As Paul says in Galatians 1:11, 12 "But I make known to you, brethren, that the gospel which was preached by me is not according to man. [12] For I neither received it from man, nor was I taught *it*, but *it came* through the revelation of Jesus Christ." Paul was an Apostle in the same way that the other 12 were Apostles because he had witnessed the risen Christ. As he says in I Corinthians 15:8 "After that He was seen by James, then by all the apostles. [8] Then last of all He was seen by me also, as by one born out of due time." Paul claims his Apostleship with humility as he says in the next verse "For I am the least of the apostles, who am not worthy to be called an apostle, because I persecuted the church of God." Paul relies on his spiritual encounter with the glorified Christ in the same way that Peter did on the Mount of Transfiguration to give evidence for his testimony.

The Light of Christ Appears to Paul

The Apostle Paul saw Christ as a glorious light which is stated in the three accounts in Acts. One that is the most interesting is in Acts 26:13 where he is giving his account to King Agrippa. "at midday, O king, along the road I saw a light from heaven, brighter than the sun, shining around me and those who journeyed with me." He is using this to give his testimony of how he became a Christian which was through his NDE-like experience. Notice that Christ appeared to him in a light brighter than the sun itself which is what many near-death experieners have reported. It's a light more brilliant than the sun but in most cases, it did not hurt their eyes. Sometimes the light is Christ specifically, and sometimes just a general intense Light that is radiating.

Paul's Shared Experience with his Companions

Those that accompanied Paul on his journey partly shared in his experience. There's some controversy about what exactly they saw and heard. Depending on the translation you read, there can appear to be a contradiction in the accounts in Acts.

In Acts 9:7 it says " And the men who journeyed with him stood speechless, hearing a voice but seeing no one" while Acts 22:9 says "And those who were with me indeed saw the light [a] and were afraid, but they did not hear the voice of Him who spoke to me." In one verse it says no voice was heard while another passage says that they did in fact hear a voice. The issue may be resolved in one of two ways. First, the men may have heard a sound but not the actual words being spoken. Another possibility is that they heard the voice and the actual words but could not understand them. We get a possible clue in Acts 26:14 "And when we all had fallen to the ground, I heard a voice speaking to me and saying in the Hebrew language, 'Saul, Saul, why are you persecuting Me." It might be that the companions did not speak or understand Hebrew as Paul did and thus could not understand the voice. I think the second possibility is probably not the answer because the men were sent with Paul by the chief priests (Acts 26:12). It would be likely that they too spoke Hebrew if they came from the chief priests.

The first answer is more likely. In the NIV it says in Acts 9:7 " The men traveling with Saul stood there speechless; they heard the sound but did not see anyone." If Jesus was communicating telepathically to Paul in Hebrew, they may have only heard the sound when Christ appeared but not any words. This would be consistent with most near-death experiencers who tend to hear people on the other side telepathically.

As to what they saw, there isn't that much difficulty. They saw a light but not the image of Christ. As many NDEers merely see just a bright light. In all, they partially shared in Paul's experience. It wasn't meant for them but the fact that they saw the light and heard the sound was enough to give further confirmation that it was an authentic spiritual experience to Paul.

Something that is just starting to get more attention is what is called the shared death experience (SDE) where a caregiver or loved one in the same room experiences all or part of what the dying person is experiencing as they cross over. This helps to further confirm the reality of the NDE because these individuals are fully healthy and conscious. Paul's companions had something similar to an SDE with Paul, only one might call it a secondary STE or shared transformative experience with Jesus. I'm sure Paul shared Christ and what he experienced more fully with them later.

Paul's Transformation and Mission

The transformation of Paul was the most radical one recorded in all of scripture. Paul went from a murderer of Christians to being an Apostle of Christ. His conversion is one of the strongest testimonies for the power of Christ in the scriptures that we have. In fact, other than the resurrection, this may be the most powerful witness for the scriptures. Apologetical books have been written making the case for faith based on Paul's conversion. The change was so radical that one must conclude that Paul did have a genuine experience. Not only was the change radical, but it's doubtful that he would have made up the account because by converting to Christianity, he would lose his reputation and risk his life. This is exactly what happened to Paul on both fronts.

Near-death experiences like Paul's conversion are also filled with radical transformations. One of which was that of Dannion Brinkley. He went from a life of violence and anger to one of love and compassion much like Paul.[7] We will be looking at Dannon more throughout this book.

Paul like Moses was also given a mission from God which he was to fulfill. Christ specifically gave him his mission in Acts 26:16-18

> But rise and stand on your feet; for I have appeared to you for this purpose, to make you a minister and a witness both of the things which you have seen and of the things which I will yet reveal to you. [17] I will [b]deliver you from the *Jewish* people, as well as *from* the Gentiles, to whom I [c]now send you, [18] to open their eyes, *in order* to turn *them* from darkness to light, and *from* the power of Satan to God, that they may receive forgiveness of sins and an inheritance among those who are sanctified[d] by faith in Me

Paul's mission was unique among the Apostles in that he was going to be sent primarily to preach the gospel to the Gentiles. There had been some outreach to the gentiles by the Apostles before Paul, but the Apostles were still predominantly preaching to Jews. His encounter with Christ was to be the springboard to his ministry. Paul's ministry to the Gentiles really opened up the Great Commission which was given by Christ to go into all the world making disciples. (Mathew 28:16-20). The word Gentile means nations.

As we have said before, a sense of mission is a common theme among near-death experiencers. NDEers feel like there's a calling on their life and that their life has a purpose to fulfill.

Paul's Miracle that Followed his Damascus Experience

Paul was blinded as a result of his encounter with Christ. As it says in Acts 9:8,9 "Then Saul arose from the ground, and when his eyes were opened he saw no one. But they led him by the hand

and brought *him* into Damascus. ⁹ And he was three days without sight, and neither ate nor drank." Christ could have orchestrated this experience without blinding him, but he had a purpose in this particular situation for blinding. Paul was to meet with Ananias to receive healing. This healing would help to confirm that Christ had called Paul to his work. The church was afraid of Paul as Ananias says in Acts 9:13, 14 "Then Ananias answered, "Lord, I have heard from many about this man, how much [b]harm he has done to Your saints in Jerusalem. ¹⁴ And here he has authority from the chief priests to bind all who call on Your name." The healing may have also been a further confirmation to Paul himself that it really was Christ that he met on the road to Damascus. Paul was given a vision of Ananias coming to heal him in Acts 9:12 "And in a vision, he has seen a man named Ananias coming in and putting *his* hand on him, so that he might receive his sight." This too was a confirming miracle for Paul.

Many near-death experiencers have miracles that result from their experience. Mellen-Thomas Benedict was spontaneously healed of terminal brain cancer when he returned from his NDE.[8]

Paul's Damascus Experience May have helped to Trigger his later NDE

It's not uncommon for near-death experiencers to have had a spiritually transformative event in their lives before their NDE. Sometimes it happens in early childhood, sometimes even in infancy. They may not even remember it until having their NDE. It's also true that some people that have had NDEs go on to have an STE or other near-death experiences later on. A spiritually transformative event seems to trigger other such events in a person's life. The first event may help to connect a person to the spiritual energy from God. From that, miracles seem to follow more naturally for them.

Paul's near-death experience may have been possibly triggered by his road to Damascus encounter with Jesus. It may have also contributed to other miracles that Paul was able to perform in his ministry. In Acts 19:11, 12 it says "Now God worked unusual miracles by the hands of Paul, [12] so that even handkerchiefs or aprons were brought from his body to the sick, and the diseases left them and the evil spirits went out of them". It would appear that Paul was operating with a special connection to the power of God.

Paul and the Apostles were able to perform their miracles because they were given a special power from Christ. This is consistent with what scripture teaches. (see Luke 10:19) Christ himself operated in a power from God that came from a special connection. He knew when the woman healed with an issue of blood had touched him because he says he felt power leave him. As he says in Luke 8:46 "But Jesus said, "Someone touched me; I know that power has gone out from me."(NIV)

This special connection that the Apostles had may help to explain what we read in the book of Acts with so many miracles being able to be performed by them. This is not to say miracles do not happen today in the church, I believe they do, we just don't seem to see them with the same frequency. With the NDE today, we are starting to see some biblical-like miracles occurring which will be discussed as we progress.

3. JESUS

Many near-death experiencers met Jesus during their time on the other side and were forever changed. Some who did not know Christ before the experience actually came to know him as a result of their NDE. So many wonderful NDEs could be discussed of how Jesus transformed their life in heaven. Three astonishing ones are Howard Storm, Ian McCormick, and George Rodonaia. All three were self avowed atheists before their experiences. They come from different nations and walks of life. Howard was a college professor from the United States. Ian was a young traveling surfer living a bohemian lifestyle who was originally from New Zealand. George was a genius and dissident from the Soviet Union who was invited to speak in the US on scientific breakthroughs in psychology.

After their experience, all three went into ministry with Howard and George becoming pastors and Ian going into evangelism.

Howard Storm's NDE where he Encounters Jesus

Howard Storm had been raised in the church as a child but rejected it as he grew up. He ended up becoming a proud cynical person by the time of his NDE at the age of 38 in 1985. At times he could be a nasty person before his near-death experience.. Howard was an Art Professor working for a college in Kentucky at the time of his experience in 1985.

Howard's NDE

Howard had traveled to France with a class when he had his NDE. On the trip, he had become violently ill with a perforated stomach and needed to be transported to the hospital for medical attention. At the hospital, he died. At first, he was not aware that he had passed and was walking around outside his body. His wife came in to see his lifeless body and Howard attempted to communicate with her, but she couldn't hear him. Howard became angry. A bit later, a few people met Howard telling him that he needed to come with them. Howard assumed it was the doctors, so he went with them. He was surprised that they spoke english so well with no accent.

He arrived in a room which was dark and was subsequently attacked by them. Unbeknownst to Howard at the time, these beings were actually demons. They had initially been kind when speaking with him, but became more impatient and began to take a surly tone before the attack. After the assault, he was left in the darkness on the ground in pain suffering. The thought then occurred to him, call out to Jesus for help. He did, and immediately was rescued by Jesus and taken into the light.

Howard was given a life review where his entire life was displayed before his eyes. He was then able to dialogue with Jesus and other companions who were present. He was able to ask them many questions. One question that we already covered in a previous chapter was concerning the Bible where he was told it was divinely inspired.

Which Religion is the Right One?

Howard at one point asked which religion was the correct one. He thought a specific church or religion would be given. Instead, he was told the right religion is the one that helps you get closer to God. This answer stunned him. Angie Fenimore during her NDE asked about which religion was true and was told that "they're all true.[9] In other words, all religions have some truth and help to meet the person where they are in their spiritual journey at the time.

This isn't to say that all religions are the same or that one might not be more advanced than another, just that they can all help you to learn and grow where you are. If one religion was more advanced than another, it might not be what a person needs at that time. They may not be ready for it. If you have a five year old that hasn't completed kindergarten yet, putting him or her in a graduate studies class would be of no use to him or her.

The Uniqueness of Christ

Howard has stated that Christianity presents the clearest expression of spiritual truth out there. This is so because it revolves specifically around the person of Jesus Christ. Jesus is unique in that he is the perfect Son of God that died for our sins and rose again. He truly is the creator and firstborn of creation (See Colossians 1:15).

I can appreciate many prophets, teachers, and sages both in scripture and outside scripture, but they don't have the uniqueness that Jesus has. This would include, for example, the Apostle Peter. He was used mightily of God, and we benefit from his teachings in scriptures, but he lacks the distinctiveness of Christ. Same could be said for any religious teacher such as Buddha. Buddha has brought much enlightenment, peace, compassion, etc into the world through his life and teachings, but he didn't die for my sins.

What is interesting about Buddha, is that there is some evidence that he may have predicted the coming of Jesus in "The Golden Boat" based in a Cambodian Buddhist Manuscript. He spoke of another Buddha who would come that would be greater than him that would take away the sins and bad karma of the world.

No doubt, Jesus sent many teachers, prophets, and sages before and after to help us, but he is the ultimate one we should look to complete our spiritual journey. Christ can use people's religious and philosophical beliefs to teach them about love and start them on their spiritual path. He is the Way, but his way is love.

Many people from other faiths have seen Jesus in near-death experiences, including Jewish people. Jesus is the fulfillment of all religions in one form or another. The wise men that came from the East to see him were probably Zoasterians. In Taoism, the way or tao is the ultimate reality. The Greek word Logos in John 1:1 translated word in English Bibles is translated tao in Chinese Bibles. Jesus is the Tao or way of God.

Is there a place for the great commission? (See Matthew 28:18-20) Absolutely! We are to bring the clear picture of truth in Jesus to the whole world. Jesus is the perfect picture of how we are to love. If people don't embrace him now, we don't need to worry because they may not be ready just yet to receive greater truth. Some like Apollos in Acts 18:24-26 were prepared by the Spirit to have their understanding of the truth perfected, but many may not be ready for such a step. All we can do is share the truth and pray that they can continue to have their eyes opened to more truth.

Howard asked about other Life in the Universe

One thing I find interesting is that Howard at one point in his questioning asked about other life in the universe. He was informed that there was other life in the universe and actually other life in other universes. There are many worlds with some beings that look pretty much like humans and others that look much different.[10]

What's really fascinating is that he was told that Jesus has been to other worlds and is the savior of many worlds. This makes our picture of Jesus as Lord much grander than we ever imagined. I found this information to be thrilling!

The Bible really doesn't speak about other worlds in the universe directly. Its focus is on our own world. Are there possible illusions in scripture to them? Well, Jesus did say that he has other sheep that he needed to go to. (See John 10:16). This is definitely referring to us today as believers as well as believers all over the globe and throughout the ages. This could also be referring to other people groups that he may have visited after his resurrection. I have a couple books in my library discussing legends of him visiting people from various parts of the world including the Americas, India, China, etc. Might it also possibly be referring to other believers in other worlds? I think the answer might be yes. We may have other brothers and sisters from other worlds.

Colossians 1:20 says " and by Him to reconcile all things to Himself, by Him, whether things on earth or things in heaven, having made peace through the blood of His cross." We saw that heavens in scripture can be referring to the spiritual realm of God, but also to the universe. Why would God's realm need to be reconciled? It seems possible it may be referring to other worlds in the universe.. In I Corinthians 15, might the all things being brought under his feet refer to other worlds?

Another thing to ponder is, where did the Angels come from? We know they are created beings, but did they come from a world like our own way back that met its consummation and now they spend eternity helping worlds like our own to come to God as well as serving God? Jesus did say that we would be like the Angels (See Matthew 22:30). Maybe someday, when this world has passed away, we might effectively be Angels to a world not in existence yet, or a much younger world now. I do realize that much of this is my own speculation, but its food for thought.

Howards visions of the Future

Howard was given visions of the future during his near-death experience. Some revolve around catastrophes to come to both America and the World that will shake us to the core. This is in line with scriptures talking about times of tribulation to come to the earth (See Matthew 24:6-6, Revelation 6:9-11, 7:14) Howard also saw a time where people would live more simply in peace worldwide. The earth would be greener and people would be able to grow food or experience healing simply through prayer. This sounds like the millennial reign of Christ or the new earth (See Isaiah 2:1-5, 11:6-9, Micah 4:1-4, and Revelation 20:1-15).

Howards Transformation

Howard was profoundly transformed as a result of his NDE. He went from being an atheist to a committed Christian, and even became a pastor. Once he returned from his NDE, he had a voracious appetite to study the Bible and anything related to the Christian faith. He now ministers around the world for Christ using his NDE to testify of the Lord's glory. He was forever changed because he met Jesus in his experience, much like the Apostle Paul on the road to Damascus. Both men did a complete 180 after they were confronted by Christ.[11]

Ian McCormack, a Young Surfer Who Finds Christ

Ian was originally from New Zealand traveling to various parts of the world including Australia, New Zealand, and throughout SouthEast Asia. He had been living the surfer beach bum lifestyle on his journey for two years and in 1982 had finally come to the small island of Mauritius on the Indian Ocean.

He had gone out diving with some of his Creole Fisherman buddies when he was stung multiple times by box jellyfish. He began to feel weak and nearly passed out. The fisherman took him back to shore and left him on the beach. He was able to walk and find a taxi driver that agreed only to take him for help if Ian agreed to pay him. Instead of taking him to the hospital, the driver dumped him off close to Ian's hotel and left. Ian was spotted by a friend and taken inside the hotel where an ambulance was called. Before the ambulance was called, the owner of the hotel came up to him and saw marks on his arm and wrote him off as nothing more than a drug addict.

The Lord's Prayer

Ian was eventually taken by ambulance and while inside, almost lost consciousness. It was at this point that his NDE started. He heard God say to him that if he closed his eyes, he would never awake again. Ian was trying with all his might to stay awake but could feel that he was dying.

He began to see images of his life including being a young boy.

He then saw the face of his mother who told him that God loved him and that he should call out to him for help. Ian then called out to God, still not fully believing that he was real. He asked God to help him pray the Lord's Prayer which was the only one he could vaguely remember growing up.

He began to see the words appear before his eyes and each part took on meaning to him from his own life. God would show him different areas of his life and how they related to the prayer. This included the need to forgive others. Ian then saw the taxi driver and struggled to forgive him.

From Ian's NDE, elements of scripture would become alive to him, both during the experience and afterward.

The Realm of Darkness

Ian eventually died and found himself in a dark place not having any idea where he was. He began to hear disturbing voices telling him to shut up and that he was getting what he deserved. Ian asked these beings where he was. The beings told him he was in hell. Within a few seconds, however, the darkness completely broke.

A Place of Wonderful Light and Love

Ian found himself surrounded by a bright light that appeared to shine from all directions. It was a light brighter than any he had ever seen on earth. The Light shined in and through him and all around him. He felt that he was one with the Light. He realized it was the Light of God and the scripture that says "God is Light and in Him is no Darkness" (I John 1:5 KJV).

From the Light, he began to feel waves of unconditional abundant love. He felt so unworthy and began to think of all the sins in his life. As he did this, more and more love washed over him. He knew that God was also love. (I John 4:7)

Out of the Light came a Being of Light that shone and was wearing sandals. Ian was not sure who this Being was until after his NDE, and he believes this Being was Jesus.

The Choice

The Light opened up in the center to reveal a beautiful nature scene. Ian was then given a choice to either stay or return to his life on earth. Ian told God that he had no reason to go back and wanted to stay. He then saw an image of his mother and remembered that she would think that he died and went to hell. Ian decided to return to earth at that point.

Why Did Ian Briefly go to Hell?

Ian was told by God afterward that had he not called out to him, he would have been left in hell until the Day of Judgment. This judgment would probably have been a more complete life review than the few images of his life that he saw earlier. Many NDEers have spent what feels like hundreds or thousands of years in hell before they were taken out by God to go into the Light and have a life review. Ian spent what sounded like a few moments in darkness.

Ian probably could have been taken straight into the Light and been fine, but there may have been a reason why he needed to spend some time briefly in the darkness. It helped to picture the stark contrast between what his life was before the experience and what it became afterward as a result of it. We have passed from darkness into light (Ephesians 5:8). I believe the darkness was probably the darkness within Ian's own soul, and the demons possibly were his own inner demons. Hell is primarily a mental state within your own being, the feeling of being separated from God.

The BluePrint for Prayer

I've heard it said that the Lord's Prayer is the blueprint for all prayer. Each element establishes the template for how we should pray each day. Prayer is one of the ways we come into communion daily with God. For Ian, the Lord's Prayer which is recorded in Matthew 6:9-13 became something emphatically real to him during his experience. This is how the NDE can make the scriptures come alive for the experiencer as well as for us today. The teachings of scripture are not just nice things to believe in but have actual power for our lives. They're principles of how the universe works. The near-death experience vividly illustrates this for us.

Jesus is the Brilliant Light

Ian saw a man that had a glowing white robe with light shining from him that seemed to light up the entire universe. He wore golden sandals. Ian was not even aware that scripture has a description of Jesus in heaven that exactly matched what he saw. God gave this scripture to him after his experience. Revelations 1:13:16

> 13 and in the midst of the seven lampstands *One* like the Son of Man, clothed with a garment down to the feet and girded about the chest with a golden band. 14 His head and hair *were* white like wool, as white as snow, and His eyes like a flame of fire; 15 His feet *were* like fine brass, as if refined in a furnace, and His voice as the sound of many waters; 16 He had in His right hand seven stars, out of His mouth went a sharp two-edged sword, and His countenance *was* like the sun shining in its strength.

Again, his NDE gave him a visual representation of what is told in scripture even before he was aware of this scripture. The NDE illuminates the reality of Jesus Christ in a stunning way. What the Apostle John saw in his vision of heaven is what many NDEers like Ian have also seen to this day.

To experience the Light of Jesus in our lives, we don't need to wait until we die. As Revelations 3:20 says "Behold, I stand at the door and knock. If anyone hears My voice and opens the door, I will come in to him and dine with him, and he with Me." We may not see the dazzling light that Ian did, but we can begin to feel it within our soul. The NDE can bring great hope to us in our heart that what the scriptures teach is true.

Ian now shares his NDE to proclaim the truth of Jesus to thousands around the world each year. He truly was born of the Spirit as a result of his experience and is excited to share that in his testimony. Ian's near-death experience is one of my favorite and inspiring NDEs that I have studied over the years. I never get tired of hearing his story.[12]

George Rodonaia, from Materialist to Faith

George was originally from the former Soviet Union before he eventually moved to the United States. He was a genius and had earned doctorates in science, medicine, and psychology. In 1976 at the age of 22, he was invited to give a presentation on medical breakthroughs in psychology. He had gotten approval to leave the Soviet Union to speak but before he could leave, he was run over by a car and killed. The KGB had sought to take him out because he was part of an underground movement supporting freedom and reform in the USSR. He was rushed to the hospital but was pronounced dead when the doctors were unable to save him. He was moved to the morgue and would be dead for three days.

George was Aware in the Darkness.

During the three days that George was dead, he had a near-death experience. His experience started in total darkness. He knew he was conscious. This intrigued George because he had always been an atheistic materialist. How was it possible that he could be dead without a body and still be aware? He decided to try to think positive and then saw a light in the distance that he began to move toward. Eventually, he was fully engulfed by the Light.

Lessons in the Light

When George first came into the Light, it was painful. It felt like a huge pressure being put on him. Eventually, he got used to it and was given his life review. In the Light, he came to understand that love was everything. It was what the light was and was the purpose of life on earth. While in the Light, he never directly saw Jesus as Howard or Ian had.

Miracle in the Morgue

When George came back, he had been dead in the morgue for three days and awoke without any medical assistance. This astonished the medical staff and caused many to become Christians. Three days being dead, parallels that of Christ and is a miracle much on the order of Lazarus in scripture.

After George's NDE

After George's near-death experience, he came to faith and became interested in the study of theology. He would go on to seminary and be ordained in the Russian Orthodox Church. He later was also ordained as a Methodist minister.[13]

4. SPIRITUAL REALMS

When mentioning spiritual dimensions beyond our physical one on earth, we're speaking of heaven and hell. There may be more realms than just heaven and hell, but for our consideration, we will limit it to those two. Within heaven and hell, there're many spheres within each, probably millions or more. The reason I say this, is that we create or co-create with God and others, various realms within the two larger realms. This would make sense since we are creative beings and made in the image of our creator.

The NDE confirms that we help to form our own heaven and hell. What is in our soul can shape what we experience, for good or ill. As Christ said, "the kingdom of God is within you"(Luke 17:21). All the light or darkness in this life and the next flows from within us. "For as he thinks in his heart, so *is* he". (Proverbs 23:7)

We tend to think of heaven as up and hell as down and there seems to be some truth to that. As seen earlier, Stephan looked up and saw Christ and God in heaven.(see Acts 7:55) Jesus ascended into heaven after 40 days from his resurrection. (see Acts 1:9) Many near-death experiencers have felt the sense of moving up toward the Light as they were leaving their bodies. Sometimes it's a short trip, sometimes into outer space and beyond. It's as if a portal opens up at some point for each one passing away. A tunnel may be present which we travel through to get to the Light, but not in every case.

Things in Heaven

There are infinite things that one could potentially experience in the heavenly realms. Our focus will be on just a few shared by both scripture and the near-death experience. This is not intended to be an exhaustive list.

Structures that have been Constructed in Heaven

People have seen complete cities with temples, libraries, God's throne room, houses, gates, streets of gold, and other structures in heaven. Some such as Mellen-Thomas Benedict were given tours of various areas of heaven. In heaven, Mellen saw cities, nations, and continents. Some NDEers saw heaven as possibly even a planet.[14]

We know from many scriptures that there is at least a city in heaven. As it says in Hebrews 11:16 "But now they desire a better, that is, a heavenly *country*. Therefore God is not ashamed to be called their God, for He has prepared a city for them." This verse also references a better country that goes along with what Mellen saw of nations in heaven.

The city of heaven is often called New Jerusalem as Revelation 21:2 says "Then I, [a]John, saw the holy city, New Jerusalem, coming down out of heaven from God, prepared as a bride adorned for her husband" Its fitting in a spiritual sense that heaven would be called New Jerusalem because the city of Jerusalem on earth had such significance. I don't doubt that there's a literal city in heaven with the name New Jerusalem. Some believe that New Jerusalem is heaven itself, but I believe it's a realm within heaven and not the entire thing. The verse above says that New Jerusalem came out of heaven. Revelations goes on to lay out the exact dimensions of this city in Revelations 21:16. The city is a gigantic cube hundreds of miles in diameter from top to bottom. Whether this is a literal measurement or put there to simply show that the city is huge, I don't know. If the measurement is literal, heaven would still be much larger in that it's not limited to just the city. Plus, this was the measurement as John saw it in AD 90 approximately, it may have continued to expand over time.

People during their near-death experiences have seen homes,

sometimes large homes or mansions. In some cases, they saw their own homes which will be waiting for them when they return to heaven. The homes had a connection to how they lived on earth in that the home was built on things like love, compassion, kindness, etc. So the homes had a literal form but represented spiritual truths at the same time. Jesus said in John 14:2 "In My Father's house are many [a]mansions; if *it were* not *so,* [b]I would have told you. I go to prepare a place for you." Obviously, this has a spiritual meaning to it primarily. Heaven is called God's house, and within that house are more houses. It's a dwelling place for us. The ESV uses the word "rooms" for mansion as do other translations. The NRSV uses the term "dwelling places" in John 14:2 for mansions. Rooms or Dwellings can relate to the fact that heaven has many realms. Sometimes NDEers felt like the area of heaven they were taken too was prepared specifically just for them. It was exactly what their soul would have desired.

People have seen libraries in heaven, which the Bible doesn't specifically reference but it does mention books in heaven that are open. (Revelation 20:12). There's a book of life and books with our works. This may be spiritual as well, but take on a literal meaning as people experience heaven. If there are books, then it's reasonable to believe a library or libraries would be there. Temples also exist in heaven as NDEers have reported as it says in Revelation 11:19 " Then the temple of God was opened in heaven, and the ark of [i]His covenant was seen in His temple. And there were lightnings, noises, thunderings, an earthquake, and great hail"

One such person to be taken to a library containing the book of life during her near-death experience was Karen Thomas. She was also able to see a great temple in heaven.[15]

Many have seen the Throne of God and the gates of heaven. Dannion Brinkley saw the gates with pearls firsthand.[16] Remember Emmanuel Tuwagirairmana, he found himself at the gates of heaven and was told that the Throne of God was just on the other side. Revelations 4:2 says "Immediately I was in the Spirit; and behold, a throne set in heaven, and *One* sat on the throne. " The Throne of God is literal but it is also spiritual as it says in Isaiah 66:1 "Heaven *is* My throne". All of heaven is the realm of God.

Nature in Heaven

Many scenes in heaven actually resemble earth in terms of natural beauty. The imagery is usually just more dazzling. Whatever you can think of as something beautiful in nature is represented in heaven in one form of another. Arthur Yensen described seeing twin mountain tops that he believed looked like ones in Japan. He saw a shimmering golden lake that was breathtaking. One woman was able to see the most exquisite flowers she had ever seen. Many NDEers have seen rivers and trees and sometimes have said they saw the river and tree of life mentioned in scripture.[17] How much of what is seen is shaped by what the person wishes to see? Well, there's an element to heaven that is highly personalized. We imagine things because we are created in the image of God and are creative beings at our core. In heaven, we are more fully able to co-create with our Creator. We know that we will be ruling and reigning with Him in heaven. (See II Timothy 2:12, and Revelation 20:4-6) Part of that ruling and reigning may be in co-creating an expanding heaven.

It might also be the other way around to some extent. The beauty we see on earth may reflect what was already in heaven. Think of the Garden of Eden with lush trees, flowers, and grass with everything being perfect. We as humans have a concept of what the most perfect beautiful world would be possibly because that is where we ultimately came from. The original garden reflects our heavenly home as does nature on earth today, though to a lesser extent. This concept is much like Plato's ideal forms. We know that an ideal form of everything we see must exist somewhere whether it be a tree, flower, or lake. What is interesting about Plato, is that he was one of the earliest people in the ancient world outside of scripture to speak of a near-death experience. He wrote of a soldier named Er who crossed into the afterlife realm and came back. The description is analogous to modern NDEs.[18] Like the New Testament, Plato's thoughts most likely were influenced by the near-death experience.

Dean Braxton during his near-death experience saw each element of heaven as alive and possessing consciousness. We know that grass is alive but in heaven, it's like we can communicate with it. The rocks even seem to have some kind of life.[19] This may be true on earth, but we may have lost the awareness due to sin entering the world.

Not everyone has experienced heaven as natural scenery, sometimes it's just more of a consciousness and of being in the Light. Heaven was more ethereal for them. It can still be a wonderful experience. Nanci Danison was able to mentally shift her experience as she wished while in heaven. If she wanted a mountain scene, she could go there in a thought. If she wanted an open field, she could go there instantly. Then she could zap right back to simply being in the Light.[20] This supports the idea that we can create our experience and move to different dimensions by mere thought. This isn't to say that the places are not real, they absolutely become a reality for us, and we experience them more vividly than anything on earth, it's a hyper-reality. I actually think the idea of shaping our own heaven sounds awesome. It's sort of like having your own holodeck from star trek in the spiritual world. Heaven may be more of a mental construct but no less real in any sense of the word.

There appears to be universal agreement among near-death experiencers that there was no sun in heaven. Of all the NDEers that have commented on what lights heaven, all have said that they did not see the sun but knew that the Light of God was the one that lights up heaven. Karen said that heaven was lit by God and everything that was there. Everything such as the trees had light emanating from it. The scripture says in Revelation 21:23 "The city had no need of the sun or of the moon to shine in it, for the glory of God illuminated it. The Lamb is its light"

Pets and Animals in Heaven

Many NDEers saw pets in heaven as well as other animals. This can bring great joy to any pet owner who has lost a pet in his or her lifetime. I know that I have lost several dogs over the years as well as a few cats. Losing a pet can be a harrowingly painful experience to say the least. One dog that I'm especially looking forward to seeing again will be Quasi who was the first dog that exclusively belonged to me. Quasi was a Pomeranian that was as smart as a whip and full of life. Quasi was always there to comfort me and was my best friend during some difficult points in my life.

Jonathon G saw all his former pets, including cats and dogs when he had his near-death experience. Kathy Baker saw several dogs running in an open field during her NDE in 1985. Jonathon's and Kathy's experiences with seeing pets in heaven is reminiscent of the old "Rainbow Bridge" Poem that someone may have shared with you after the loss of a pet.[21] There's a great deal of truth in that poem! During the writing of this book, we lost our little dog Skippy and the vet's office gave our five-year old son a small coloring workbook with the poem illustrated inside. My mind instantly went to all of the NDEs where people saw their dogs in heaven. It doesn't erase the pain of losing your furry friend, but it does help give some comfort.

Sometimes pets have the ability to communicate to their owners in thoughts on the other side. I don't know how this works, it might be that the feelings of the pet are converted into words which are then sent to the person telepathically. So you may not only get to see your pet, but you may be able to talk to them in a way that you never could while on earth! The idea that animals could speak may not be so foreign to scripture, some believe that before the fall, animals may have had the ability to communicate with people in words such as the serpent did with Eve in the garden.

The Bible directly mentions certain animals being in heaven

or within God's Kingdom. Revelation 19:11 says "Now I saw heaven opened, and behold, a white horse. And He who sat on him *was* called Faithful and True". The Apostle John actually saw a horse in heaven. It's reasonable to assume other animals would be present and why not all animals who were once alive on this earth being there?

Isaiah makes specific reference to animals living in God's kingdom in peace with each other as it says in 65:25
>The wolf and the lamb shall feed together,
>The lion shall eat straw like the ox,
>And dust *shall be* the serpent's food.
>They shall not hurt nor destroy in all My holy mountain,"

>Says the Lord

God's plan of salvation through Christ always included His entire creation, including animals. As it says in Luke 3:6 "And all flesh shall see the salvation of God." God preserves both "people and animals" as it says in Psalms 36:6 (NIV). In Colossians 1:20 "and by Him to reconcile all things to Himself, by Him, whether things on earth or things in heaven, having made peace through the blood of His cross." Acts 3:21 says pretty much the same thing "whom heaven must receive until the times of restoration of all things, which God has spoken by the mouth of all His holy prophets since [e]the world began."

The creation itself will be delivered from the bondage of sin as we will be as it says in Romans 8:21, 22 "whom heaven must receive until the times of restoration of all things, which God has spoken by the mouth of all His holy prophets since [e]the world began."

Music in Heaven

Many near-death experiencers commented on the beautiful music that they heard in heaven. Jennine Wolff heard the most glorious celestial music along with seeing vivid stunning colors. The music is more exquisite than anything on earth.[22] Music on earth that's the closest to the music in heaven seems to be new age or ambient music which has a very relaxing tranquil quality. We know from the scripture that music will be a part of heaven. (See Revelation 14:2, 3) One instrument that is mentioned is the harp. The harp plays beautiful tranquil music and that has been around for thousands of years. David played the harp for Saul (I Samuel 16:14-23). Unformituely, the fact that harps are mentioned, the idea grew that the only thing we would be doing in heaven is sitting on a cloud playing the harp which is not true.

The Silver Cord

Some near-death experiencers such as Dr. Dianne Morrissey saw a silver cord attached to her as she was leaving her body. The cord can be attached to people at different locations on the body.[23] This cord can appear elastic and shine with light. It does tend to be golden or silver and shimmering, resembling a phone cord. The silver cord is mentioned in scripture in Ecclesiastes 12:6 "Remember your Creator before the silver cord is loosed". This may connect us in this world to the spiritual realm. Once the cord is severed, a person can't go back to their physical body.

This silver cord is much like the umbilical cord. Once it's cut, we're then birthed into a new world. One would assume that in some way, NDEers never lost connection to this cord though it may not have always been in sight. The cord is of a spiritual quality that isn't always visible. Since the cord was attached for near-death experiencers, this may be why some were able to call out to Christ and be saved from hell. Death had not entirely set in yet.

The New Heaven

The scriptures teach of a new heaven in verses such as Revelation 21:1. I have always wondered why a perfect realm like heaven would ever need to pass away or disappear. If it's perfect already then why would it need to give way to a new perfect heaven? This always baffled me. I think when speaking of passing away though, it may not mean that it completely disappears but is rather continuously being transformed and expanded upon.

This concept would fit with our co-creative activities in heaven. Heaven in a sense is constantly being remade and is expanding out. Thus, the new heaven in that sense is not a completely different heaven to come in the future but a present tense heaven that is always transforming. This is my own thought, so one can take it with a grain of salt. All of what the Apostle John saw in Heaven is there but it may have been dramatically added to and some of it may have been remodeled so to speak. That's why so many NDEers see biblical imagery.

The Realms of Hell

Like heaven, hell can take many forms and be experienced in different ways by NDEers. Hell can be a place of complete darkness or can be a gray dreary place. It can have the traditional imagery of fire and brimstone or be earthbound realms where you wander the earth unable to physically experience anything or satisfy your cravings. Ghosts are real states that people can live in according to some near-death experiencers which is hellish. These are usually people that are lost or afraid to go into the light. For the discussion here, the focus will be on the dark realms and the fiery ones which appear both in scripture and the near-death experience.

The Void

The realm of extreme darkness that some near-death experiencers encounter is called the void. Beyond the darkness which can be terrifying enough, is the feeling of loneliness and despair. In a few cases, people have been in total darkness but felt the presence of God there which can make all the difference. If God is there, it can still be heavenly, if not, it can be the worst hell imaginable. The feeling of separation from God and His love is unbearable and heartbreaking.

Angie Fenimore descended into the void after her life review which is unusual in that most NDEers that get rescued out of this horrifying realm experience the Light and a life review after being in darkness. Angie had been a low point in her life emotionally and committed suicide which caused her to die and have her experience. Hell and this dark realm much like heaven is crafted by our own soul and expectations. Angie has stated that the darkness is a product of the emotional trauma and darkness within.[24] The more you walk in love, the closer you are to Christ and the more light you experience. The further you walk in ways contrary to love, the more darkness you will experience. Heaven and hell are not just realms you experience after you die physically but can be experienced in this lifetime. It's just when you die, you begin to live more fully out of your soul and the sensations take on a higher level of reality. Suicide is one of those things that can bring you into great darkness, and you're in a dark place when you begin to consider such a thing. The Kingdom of God is within you but so too can be a kingdom of darkness.

The Bible mentions this place of darkness in a few passages, which is referred to as outer darkness. Jesus said in Mathew 22:13 "Then the king said to the servants, 'Bind him hand and foot, [b] take him away, and cast *him* into outer darkness; there will be weeping and gnashing of teeth." The picture is of the King pushing the person into darkness, but ultimately, we propel ourselves into this darkness.

Fire and Brimstone

Only a few NDEers experience a place of fire and brimstone. Occasionally even demons will be present. The fire I don't believe is a literal physical fire but is a reality generated by the person or is co-created with others. It's an expectation of what hell is supposed to be for them. When Christ spoke of a fiery hell in verses such as Mathew 25:46, he was speaking most likely of an allegorical fire that is for purification. We will delve into this fire later in this book.

The Demons when they appear can be actual dark spirits, I do believe there are literal demons that exist. In most cases, however, they're probably personifications of the darkness within a person's soul. Fear, greed, lust, etc can take the form of a hideous being to torment a person within the hellish realms. Luckily, even most hellish experiences don't involve demons or places of fire. Hellish NDEs only represent a small minority of near-death experiences. This may be because many will come to the Light of God or call out to Christ and be saved before total death has set in. In most cases, the silver cord has not been completely severed at clinical death.

5. LOVE

Much could be said about love as it relates to the near-death experience and the Bible. It can be difficult to know where to start. As far as both are concerned, there's nothing more important to either than love. Virtually every positive near-death experiencer discusses the overwhelming feeling of love and how it's central to God and our purpose on earth. Love is the most powerful element in the NDE and everything else. Love is discussed so much in our society including songs, movies, TV, and books that it's easy to tune out. Many people take a flippant dismissive attitude to the subject. "Oh yeah, love, love is great" they might say.

Part of the problem might be that when we speak of love, people instantly think of the warm fuzzies that you feel with it. Love can feel wonderful, no doubt, but it's way beyond a wonderful feeling and can be present even when the feeling is not.

The best way to discuss love in scripture and the NDE is to keep it short, sweet, and simple. It's one of those things that isn't difficult to understand but takes a great deal of meditation and reflection on for most of us.

Sharon Milliman's Near-Death Experience

One could discuss virtually any NDE and have great insights to say about love. I will end up discussing more examples of how love transformed people in the near-death experience as we progress in this book. For now, let's look at Sharon Milliman. Sharon had four near-death experiences. The first one was brief due to a drowning where she hovered over her body in the water and was held by the Light. The next three were more detailed, where she met Jesus and was able to converse with him in a scenic natural setting before being taken to a beautiful city.

Besides meeting Jesus, she met two brothers that had passed away as babies but were now fully grown as well as a friend and his father. The friend's father was in the fourth NDE, and she was unaware of his passing just before her last near-death experience. She found out after coming back of his passing which gave further confirmation to her that her experience was genuine.

Lessons on Love from Sharon's NDE

The first lesson that Sharon learned from her NDE was that God's love was unconditional and that he completely accepted her. This is true for every single person, we are loved without conditions and have His total acceptance. This is such a powerful thing when you start to ponder it. You never need to worry about measuring up or if God is going to condemn you. You don't have to mire in your past mistakes and feel shame. We can simply embrace His love and feel His love and acceptance for us. Think of the Apostle Paul, he was a murderer of Christians before he embraced Christ, yet, he was fully accepted and used by God to reach millions with God's love. Few of us have ever done anything approaching actual murder, so this should give anyone hope.

Another lesson that Sharon received was that even the small things that are done in love matter and are actually the most important. When you give someone a smile or spend a little time with someone that needs you. You put your arm around someone to let them know you care. These make a tremendous difference in God's economy. This makes me think of when Jesus praised the widow for giving her two mites in the collection. (Luke 21:1-4) This mite was probably only worth a few pennies in our money today, but she gave all that she had and from a heart of love. I also think of when Jesus said that if you give a cup of cold water in his name you will be rewarded. (Mathew 10:42) I have always loved this scripture even as a child because it's something that we can all do, give something minuscule in Christ's name or out of a place of love and God will reward us. The reward might partly be the great feeling knowing that you responded in kindness towards another person.

Sharon had a life review during her near-death experience where she was able to see how her actions impacted other people. She didn't feel judged or condemned but it was a great learning experience for her to take back. The focal point of her life review was love. This is true for nearly every other NDEer. How did you treat others? Did you respond in kindness or cruelty? Were you indifferent towards others?

This is so essential to grasp. Love is central to everything we think, say, and do. I've never read an NDE where the focus was on the person's achievements. Nor, have I ever read one where the focus was on the fine points of his or her theology. Too many Christians overemphasize theology and make judgments of others or organizations based on their doctrines. Many exclusive groups will tell you if you're aren't part of our group or believe as they do, you're on the outs with God and are going to hell or will at least not make it to heaven.

You will never find an NDE where someone was turned away because they had an improper view of the Trinity or were baptized the wrong way. You will never find someone rejected by God because the prayer they prayed to receive Christ was missing key elements of doctrine. The whole focus on exacting theology is misguided and a waste of time. God's not as doctrinaire as some of us tend to think. The focal point should be on love and only issues that revolve around love. That's enough to be concerned about in this life for sure. This isn't to say there is no value in studying theology, it's just that it should not be our focal point in life, and we shouldn't use it to condemn others.

The final lesson Sharon learned about love was the ripple effect that love has on others. Our actions affect not only those we come directly into contact with but everyone they come into contact with and so on. This is true for loving and unloving actions, so we need to be thoughtful in how we treat others and how we live our lives.[25]

The ripple effect may also be one that has an eternal consequence for a person. Jesus taught us to store up our treasures in heaven rather than on earth. (Luke 12:33, 34) The main way we store up treasure in heaven is by showing love and kindness to others.

God is Love

We know from scripture that God is love (I John 4:8). It's important to realize that God IS love, not simply that God has love. The essence of His being is love. Many NDEers will attest to the fact that the core of God is pure love. It's a tangible quality that can be experienced in God. Everything in the universe is connected to love in one form or another. There's no end to this love, as it says in Psalm 136:1 "O give thanks unto the Lord; for he is good: for his mercy endureth for ever." (KJV)

Love is Everything

Love is the only thing that ultimately matters in this world and without it, nothing else matters. Paul made this point abundantly clear in I Corinthians 13:1-4

> If I speak in the tongues of men and of angels, but have not love, I am a noisy gong or a clanging cymbal. ² And if I have prophetic powers, and understand all mysteries and all knowledge, and if I have all faith, so as to remove mountains, but have not love, I am nothing. ³ If I give away all I have, and ᵈif I deliver up my body to be burned,¹ but have not love, I gain nothing. (ESV)

Notice that having all faith without love is of no value. Many Christians make faith the most critical thing, and by that, they usually mean a certain theological understanding, yet, scripture teaches that love is the most important. In fact, Paul goes on in verse 13 to say " So now faith, hope, and love abide, these three; but the greatest of these is love." It's better to have "bad" theology but love than to have perfect theology and lack love.

Paul in the same chapter in verse 8 states that love never fails,

"Love never ends. As for prophecies, they will pass away; as for tongues, they will cease; as for knowledge, it will pass away." If God is love then His love never ends as well.

God's Love is for Everyone

Barbara Springer who had a near-death experience has stated that God loves everyone without exception, and He loves them specifically regardless of who they are or what they believe.[26] This is in complete agreement with the scriptures. The most famous verse in the Bible, John 3:16 says "For God so loved the world that he gave his only begotten Son, that whosoever believeth in him should not perish, but have everlasting life".(KJV) The Bible also says in Romans 5:8 "But God demonstrates His own love toward us, in that while we were still sinners, Christ died for us." The cross itself is the supreme demonstration of His love. Sacrifice is one of the most powerful ways you can show love to someone else. I believe a massive explosion of love was released when Jesus died on the cross that was efficacious in washing away sin. I can't explain it, but this is what I feel in my spirit. When we show forth love, especially sacrificial love, we spiritually connect with the cross.

The Law of Love

Remember from Sharon' NDE, love is what matters when your life is being reviewed at death. Mathew 22:37-40 says "[37] Jesus said to him, '"You shall love the Lord your God with all your heart, with all your soul, and with all your mind.' [38] This is *the* first and great commandment. [39] And *the* second *is* like it: 'You shall love your neighbor as yourself.' [40] On these two commandments hang all the Law and the Prophets." The entire basis of the moral law is contained by love. If this is the case, what really is sin? Sin is anything contrary to love. When you sin, you miss the mark of love. Love truly is the royal law. (James 2:8)

Love can Transform Us

One of the most powerful ways people are transformed through their near-death experience is through the power of love. When a person is able to feel a tidal wave of love flowing from God on them in the Light, this can change everything about them. They are released from fear, hatred, pride, anger, jealousy, and virtually any other vise out there. Christ showed forth his power in his teachings and miracles, but more importantly, he showed his love. He fed people; healed them, and raised people from the dead giving them back to their loved ones.

Sometimes even small acts of kindness can soften a heart, as it says in Proverbs 15:1 "A gentle answer turns away wrath, but a harsh word stirs up anger." (NIV) Jesus taught to return kindness for hostility, as it says in Matthew 5:44 "But I say to you, love your enemies, bless those who curse you, do good to those who hate you, and pray for those who spitefully use you and persecute you,". Besides being the morally right thing to do, it may also help to soften and change the heart of someone filled with anger and hatred. Love in action can truly convert the soul.

Jesus taught that God loves us in that he deeply cares for us. He loved the birds of the air and the lilies of the field by caring for them (Matthew 6:26-33), but he loves us even more than that.

What is the opposite of love? It's not hatred but fear. One quality that NDEers have lost is a fear of death. Not that they're reckless in how they live, in fact, they tend to have more gratitude in and for their life. But once love comes in, the power of fear is entirely gone. As it says in I John 4:18 "There is no fear in love; but perfect love casts out fear, because fear involves torment. But he who fears has not been made perfect in love." This is one of my favorite verses in scripture. I have meditated on it often over the years. Once you begin to operate in love, the fears begin to leave your life.

God's Love is Released through His Grace

What makes Christianity distinct as a faith? The difference is the centrality of grace. It isn't that other faiths utterly lack the concept of grace, but it's not a predominant theme as in Christianity. Christianity teaches that God wishes to simply give us his grace without having to do anything to earn it. As it says in Ephesians 4:7 "But to each one of us grace has been given as Christ apportioned it."(NIV) God simply wants to shower us with His love, peace, compassion, kindness, and blessings.

This seems to fit with the near-death experience. People simply are embraced by God's love and feel the overwhelming love, joy, and peace. This isn't to say God would in any way force his grace on you, you always have the ability to say no. I have heard many NDEers say that they felt so unworthy of such love and compassion but have never read one say that they rejected it. I still believe that it would have been theoretically possible to reject it though. Interestingly, the writer of the New Testament who is known for speaking of grace the most is the Apostle Paul who had a near-death experience himself.

Grace is closely connected to Love in that it is the vehicle by which love is poured out to a person by God. The reason God gives grace is out of His love. Faith is also closely connected to both grace and love. Faith is to trust or embrace the love through grace that God is seeking to give us. Our faith must be rooted in love or it will not accomplish anything.

6. LIGHT

Much of the discussion about the Light within near-death experiences is about the literal Light that you see during the experience. There's also the perceptual Light that many saw within the scriptures during their spiritual experiences such as Peter, Jame, and John on the Mount of Transfiguration. This, of course, is an important and interesting aspect of both experiences. It's something that this book discusses throughout. In this chapter, we will be looking primarily at the spiritual aspects of the Light. Who is the Light and what does the Light do?

Who is the Light?

The Light, of course, is God, most of us understand. Christ is also the Light and the Son of God. What many don't know is that we are also the Light. Light comes from us, but we're also connected to the greater Light which is God. Sometimes near-death experiencers and people within scripture experienced aspects of the Light which may have been God, Christ, themselves or others. God was always present, I believe but sometimes our awareness is focused on a specific entity or entities within the Light.

God is the Light

In I John 1:5 it says " This is the message which we have heard from Him and declare to you, that God is light and in Him is no darkness at all." God is light, but what does it mean that in him there's no darkness? This is referring to the spiritual aspect of darkness more than the literal darkness that you would experience with your eyes? Darkness in this context is anything contrary to God's nature which is love. Any quality that doesn't align with love is that darkness.

I've actually read a few near-death experiences where the person was in complete darkness, didn't see any light, but still felt a warm peaceful loving presence with them which they generally believed to be God. The literal Light was not present, but God's spiritual Light was. Often, the literal Light does come later for them. Not everyone feels the loving presence in the void, in that situation, it can be a terrifying experience. The void without God can be a true hell, but with God, it can be heaven. The presence of God is what is more important than the darkness itself.

Pam Reynolds asked her grandmother during her NDE, whether the Light she saw was God. Her grandmother told her that the Light was only the breath of God.[27] In other words, the literal Light that one sees on the other side is merely an aspect of God. It's not God in His totality. This points to the deeper spiritual reality of the Light of God.

Jesus is the Light

Jesus is also said to be the Light in scripture, as it says in John 8:12 "Then Jesus spoke to them again, saying, "I am the light of the world. He who follows Me shall not walk in darkness, but have the light of life." Jesus is the spiritual Light of this world and if you follow him, you will not walk in spiritual darkness or outside of love. Some NDEers have been able to see and experience two Lights, that of Jesus and the Father. One such person was Betty Eadie.[28] Jesus is distinct from the Father, yet connected. Jesus gives a human face to God and what God is like. It can be difficult to think of God only in a vague spiritual sense without the human picture of Christ. He is our model of how we are to be Lights in this world and beyond.

We are the Light

We're Lights in this world and also are part of the greater Light of God, as Christ said in Matthew 5:14, 15 "You are the light of the world. A city that is set on a hill cannot be hidden. [15] Nor do they light a lamp and put it under a basket, but on a lampstand, and it gives light to all *who are* in the house." Some during the near-death experience knew and saw that they had a brilliant light within them, but also knew that the Light of Christ and God was a greater Light than their own. They also knew that their light was a part of the greater Light of God. The literal light that we are on the other side points to the spiritual reality that we are spiritual beings of love.

Not only are we a light from God, but we are also supposed to be a light to other people as Jesus went on to say in Matthew 5:16 "Let your light so shine before men, that they may see your good works and glorify your Father in heaven." As those in the world begin to glorify God, their own light begins to shine and this, in turn, can light the way for other people. Letting our light shine before others will have a ripple effect. Just as all our actions do as confirmed by the near-death experience.

What does the Light Mean for Us?

What the Light means for us can have many aspects which include truth, love, peace, joy, life, and healing. These characteristics are more fully realized as we embrace the ultimate Light which is God.

The Light is Truth and reveals it to Us

The Light can reveal the truth about ourselves, including the elements we would care not to have revealed such as our shortcomings as it says in John 3:19, 20 "And this is the condemnation, that the light has come into the world, and men loved darkness rather than light, because their deeds were evil. [20] For everyone practicing evil hates the light and does not come to the light, lest his deeds should be exposed." This goes into what NDEers experience with their life review where their whole life is laid out before them. The Light of God can also begin to reveal who we are in this lifetime. Not only our shortcomings but why we do the things that we do, and why other people are the way they are. This is why Jesus came because the people were in darkness but now they had a great Light to lead them into truth. (Mathew 4:16)

The Light is also revealed in the teachings of God as it says in Psalms 119:105 "Your word *is* a lamp to my feet And a light to my path." The scriptures are a light from God to guide us in this lifetime.

The Light Gives Love to Us

The connection between love and light in both scripture and the near-death experience is obvious to anyone who looks at it. In I John 2:9,10 it says " He who says he is in the light, and hates his brother, is in darkness until now. [10] He who loves his brother abides in the light, and there is no cause for stumbling in him." To walk in the Light will cause us to love, and one cannot help but to love while being in the Light. It's in the Light of God that we feel his love. The two are intertwined and can't be separated.

The Light Gives Peace

When we are in the Light of God, we experience a great peace. As it says in Philippians 4:7 "and the peace of God, which surpasses all understanding, will guard your hearts and minds through Christ Jesus." This peace is able to protect us and to give us understanding. A common feeling many NDEers had in the Light beyond unconditional love was a feeling of great peace, that everything was going to be alright. Being in a peaceful state can help us to see things more clearly which can be part of the understanding that God gives us, in this state it's easier to hear the voice of God within. It's in the stillness we more fully experience God. (Psalm 46:10) This immense peace is something that Ian had felt when he was in the Light during his *NDE*.[29]

The Light Give Joy

The Light can bring joy to a person, to the point of being euphoric at times. As I Peter 1:8 says "Though you have not seen him, you love him; and even though you do not see him now, you believe in him and are filled with an inexpressible and glorious joy " (NIV) If the joy is inexpressible for those that have not seen the Light of Christ, think how much more joy must be when we are in the actual presence of Christ in heaven.

Many NDEers have expressed feelings of being in absolute bliss while in the Light. Beyond any joy experienced on earth. They know the overwhelming love on the other side, but so to can be the joy and peace that one experiences. Tricia Barker felt incredible joy upon leaving her body during her near-death experience. She was surprised to realize that we survive physical death and don't truly die when the body dies.[30]

The Light Gives Life

We saw in John 8:12 that the Light of Christ brings forth life, but Christ also said that he would give us abundant life in John 10:10 "I have come that they may have life, and that they may have *it* more abundantly." Our life comes from God. He is our connection to living a more full life. Outside of God, we merely exist. During the near-death experience, people tend to feel more alive and aware on the other side than life on earth, they experience a hyper-reality that makes earth's life feel like a dream. This is what Dr. Eben Alexander experienced, a reality that felt too real compared to life on earth. It was more vivid than real life.[31]

The Light is a Healing Force

In Isaiah 58:8 says "Then your light shall break forth like the morning, Your healing shall spring forth speedily". The Light of God has a healing element to it, not just physical healing but emotional and spiritual healing. Many near-death experiencers have come back having experienced a physical healing and sometimes an emotional one as well. They feel transformed and set free from the past. This is the essence of the new creation life in Christ (II Corinthians 5:17).

I personally am beginning to understand how important the emotional healing from the love and light of God really is. We all have negative limiting beliefs that started when we were young children. It may be messages we got from our parents, whether consciously or unconsciously. We need to let God's light and love purify us. This can include taking inspiration from scripture and the NDE but can come from many other sources. God is not limited to what He can use.

7. JUDGMENT

What are the parallels between the Bible and the near-death experience concerning the subject of judgment? The two actually complement each other quite well. Within the NDE community, the judgment of a person is called the life review. Let's start with the life review and then see how the Bible fits within it.

The Life Review, The Good; The Bad; and The Ugly firsthand

NDEers commonly report having a complete review of their life as part of their experience. During the life review, every aspect of your life is played before your eyes. It can take many forms but most describe something looking like a movie screen that presents their entire life from start to finish. In some cases, near-death experiences only show highlights, but most see their entire life in vivid detail.

There's a focus on your interactions with others and how that affected them. This can include both people and in some cases, animals. You see how that person felt from their point of view. You experience any pain or joy that your actions or words caused them; the good; the bad; and the ugly. All your actions, whether positive or negative are displayed before you. You not only see how it impacted the person at that moment but how it affected them possibly throughout their life and how it affected others down the line. You begin to understand the ripple effect of your words and actions.

We Judge Ourselves

Virtually every NDEer says that they didn't feel judged by God during the NDE, that they were judging themselves during the life review. For years, I always wondered why this was so, it would seem to contradict the Bible where God is our Judge. As it says in II Timothy 4:1 "I charge *you* therefore before God and the Lord Jesus Christ, who will judge the living and the dead at His appearing and His kingdom"

There might be a clue in Romans 14:10 when it says "But why do you judge your brother? Or why do you show contempt for your brother? For we shall all stand before the judgment seat of[a] Christ" God is the Judge in the sense that we are in His courtroom so to speak, and Christ is presiding over the proceedings. Why would God actually need to read us the riot act? Think about it, everything is going to be laid bare before us, we will have nowhere to hide when God shines the spotlight on our life. All our defenses will be gone, and we will see clearly for ourselves what we did. The conscience that God gave us will be able to work perfectly with no filters. So, God is judging us but more in a subtle fashion by allowing us to see the truth for ourselves, no need for explanation.

We Don't Get Away with Anything

If we're going to experience all the ill we caused others as they experienced as well as the pain and anguish caused to others indirectly, we really don't get away with anything. This would include rapists, murderers, child molesters, etc. Think about the worst thing you can think of that one person has done to another, and that's what he or she can look forward to in the life review. If a man rapes, tortures, and murders a little girl, he's going to feel everything she experienced at his hand. Plus, he may also experience the grief he caused her family and other loved ones.

I think of people that were in the business of inflicting pain on other people day in and day out. Such as a mobster whose job was to rough people up, basically, torture them. What about the person responsible for inflicting torture on people at a concentration camp or gulag? I wouldn't want to be in their shoes at death.

I can remember watching a movie set during the time of slavery where a slave owner had a slave brutally whipped, I said to myself "I wouldn't want your life review".

Knowing that we don't get away with it has helped to take away the desire for vengeance for people that do unspeakable evil in this world. You talk about hell, this might be the worst hell you may have to face. It's possibly your lake of fire to go through. Our God is a consuming fire. (See Deuteronomy 4:24)

What about the average person who hasn't done something hideous such as murder or torture? We aren't off the hook either. We will see what our actions and words brought to others as well. Think of all those cruel words you've spoken to people in your life? I can remember a few in high school. An insult or a derogatory comment you gave someone. It may not have seemed like a big deal at the time, but you may see that it haunted that other person for years or even a lifetime. It may have negatively influenced how they interacted with others.

I have wondered if in Christ, he might take some of the pain away we experience in our life review. I do believe that if we have dealt with the issue and repented, we might not see it or at least if we do see it, we might be spared some of the torment it caused. Christ might sort of soften the blow. I do remember hearing an NDE where a woman seems to have been spared the grief she caused others in her life review for actions she had already repented of in her lifetime. I also know that in some life reviews, Christ is present with the person and actually gives comfort to them as their life review is played, he puts a loving arm around them.

Tricia Barker's Life Review

There are so many life reviews that could be looked at but one that stands out is Tricia Barker. She experienced all the good and bad she caused others, but she actually saw into the hearts and minds of people, sometimes ones she didn't consider as important or only briefly knew. She could see how many of her superficial judgments were so wrong. She could see their spiritual connections to God and how God deeply loved and cared for each person.

She was shown the importance of looking more deeply into the hearts of people rather than the shallow exterior things such as money, accomplishments, and physical appearances. She could see how her thinking had been so limited. She didn't feel judged by God, but she did feel that He was guiding the process and helping her to see and focus on what was most important for her.[32] This goes along with Proverbs 21:2 which says 'Every way of a man *is* right in his own eyes, But the Lord weighs the hearts".

That's one thing to keep in mind, the life review isn't just to point out faults, but to help us learn and grow spiritually. The life review has been one of the most transformative experiences for many NDEers.

Practicing the Life Review Now

You don't have to wait to start benefiting from the Life Review. You can start to do a life review on yourself from time to time. It will not be as vivid, and you will most certainly miss things, but it could be something that helps you on your spiritual walk. I have repented of things doing this. Paul encourages such self-reflection when he says in Galatians 6:4 "But let each one examine his own work, and then he will have rejoicing in himself alone, and not in another"

What does the Bible say about the Judgment?

We will give an account of our life to God. In Romans 14:11,12 it says "For it is written:"*As* I live, says the Lord, Every knee shall bow to Me, And every tongue shall confess to God." [12] So then each of us shall give account of himself to God. Paul is quoting Isaiah 45:23 in the passage above. So we will give an account before God of how we lived our lives? How will this account take place? The scriptures say that the books will be opened as it says in Revelation 20:12 " And I saw the dead, small and great, standing before [a]God, and books were opened. And another book was opened, which is *the Book* of Life. And the dead were judged according to their works, by the things which were written in the books".

The works we have done refers to how we lived our lives and most certainly, how we treated other people. This is consistent with the life review. Notice it says books, most NDEers describe the life review as appearing more like a movie though some did see a visual type book open up. We have to understand that the Bible was written within the personal, cultural, and religious context of the author and his audience. When scripture was written, they didn't have movies or TV so to describe it in that way would have made no sense. Plus, God can put the life review within a format that the person can comprehend. I'm sure that more people before the advent of movies and TV saw their life open up as a visual book.

The Light of Christ in Judgment

I like what John 3:19 says concerning judgment " And this is the judgment: the light has come into the world, and people loved the darkness rather than the light because their works were evil." (ESV) This is speaking specifically of Christ coming into the world but can also be applied to our judgment at death. Notice that the Light is put on us like a spotlight that exposes everything, including our sins. This fits nicely with the life review.

The next verse says "For everyone who does wicked things hates the light and does not come to the light, lest his works should be exposed." This goes along with the fact that we don't get away with anything, you're going to feel all the awful things you inflicted on others and those they impact as a result of it. You may also experience the hurt you indirectly caused their family and friends.

What will judge us according to the Bible

Jesus told the Jews that he would not judge them but Moses would in John 5:45 "Do not think that I shall accuse you to the Father; there is one who accuses you--Moses, in whom you trust." This would be the law that will judge them, such as the 10 commandments. Notice, Jesus says that he will not accuse them which goes along with God not judging us.

Jesus said that he does not judge someone for not believing in John 12:47 "And if anyone hears My words and does not [g]believe, I do not judge him; for I did not come to judge the world but to save the world". Jesus is not going to judge or condemn us. Jesus went on to say in the next verse "He who rejects Me, and does not receive My words, has that which judges him—the word that I have spoken will judge him in the last day." The words he gave will judge us, that is the testimony of love will judge to our hearts the truth.

If a person does not have the law, the scriptures teach that his own conscience will judge him as it says in Roman's 2:14-16

> for when Gentiles, who do not have the law, by nature do the things in the law, these, although not having the law, are a law to themselves, [15] who show the work of the law written in their hearts, their conscience also bearing witness, and between themselves *their* thoughts accusing or else excusing *them*) [16] in the day when God will judge the secrets of men by Jesus Christ, according to my gospel.

God doesn't need to tell us at the judgment which deeds were evil and which were good, we know the truth in our hearts.

The Judgment functions as an Assessment rather than a Condemnation by God

In John 3:17 it says "For God did not send His Son into the world to condemn the world, but that the world through Him might be saved." The role of Jesus is not condemnation but is helping us to assess the truth more clearly.

God will in some cases allow for correction at the judgment but it's not about retribution but is to be restorative as we will see in the chapter on salvation.

Salvation Before, At, or even After Judgment

One passage you will hear constantly being thrown out to say that restoration to God after death is not possible is Hebrews 9:27 which says "And as it is appointed for men to die once, but after this the judgment." Notice, nowhere does it say that salvation is made impossible at or after the judgment, it simply tells us that a judgment occurs. If the judgment is primarily to help us to learn and grow rather than being a sentencing phase, then really, there shouldn't be an issue at all.

Scientists are starting to view death as a process rather than something that is instantaneous. Many NDEers go into the Light and feel the Love of God there before the life review even starts, so they could be coming to the Lord before judgment but before death is completed which would make this verse a nonissue even from the perspective of those that believe it teaches no salvation after death.

Dr. Mary Neal was told during her near-death experience that everyone is given at least one final chance after death to receive or reject Christ. When this final offer is given we don't know, it may not be at the same time or place for every person.[33] I personally have read her book "To Heaven and Back" and was greatly blessed by it. She was a committed Christian before her NDE and grew closer to the Lord after it.

Some NDEers go straight into the Light while others go to a dark hellish place first before being rescued by the Light. This occurs before the life review starts generally speaking, so salvation is still coming before judgment. In one case that I'm aware of, the person had her life review and then descended into a dark hell before being rescued. Angie Fenimore, who we looked at earlier, had her life review and then descended into a dark hell. At a point, she saw a light coming for her. Both God the Father and Jesus were present and asked her if this was what she really wanted. She was then saved out of hell.[34] II Peter 3:18-20 is consistent with her testimony of someone being saved out of hell. Jesus actually saved people out of hell in that passage.

8. SALVATION

What is salvation and does it have anything to do with the near-death experience or only the Bible? It has relevance to both. Christians tend to speak of being saved from hell or destruction which is part of what salvation encompasses, but salvation is much more than that. Being saved from hell is only a byproduct of salvation. It's also only a negative thing we're being spared from. Salvation at its core is overwhelmingly positive. Salvation is ultimately about being restored to God. Other words sometimes used are reconciliation or redemption. (See Titus 2:14 and I Peter 5:10) If we are restored or redeemed, it implies we were once with God does it not? Yes, in the beginning, humanity was one with God but we fell away into darkness spiritually.

You must be Born Again

Being made one with God is the essence of salvation. Jesus prayed that we would all be one with each other as well as him and his Father. (See John 7:21-23) Many NDEers such as Ian McCormack have expressed that they felt profound oneness with God during their experience.[35]

Someone can become one with God through Christ but how does this happen? It's as Jesus said, "You must be born again" (John 3:3). To be born again is to be born of the Spirit. When you're born of the Spirit you are immersed in God's love and light. If you aren't immersed in that love and light, you will never experience a profound transformation, or as it says in II Corinthians 5:17, you will not become a "new creation" where "all things have become new".

How is it that someone who dies as a nonbeliever can have a

heavenly wonderful NDE? They haven't been born of the Spirit yet? I had wondered about this myself for many years. The answer came to me one day. Many who go into the Light and feel God's unconditional love are actually having their born again moment right there in the Light. A few weeks after coming to this realization, it was confirmed in a book I was reading by Kenneth Ring called "Lessons from the Light " where a person said that she now understood what Christians meant by being reborn. This person had felt that rebirth in the Light.[36] Ian said he was told when he returned to earth from his NDE that he was now a reborn Christian.

Dannion Brinkley had a profound near-death experience where he was struck by lightning in 1975 and was pronounced dead. He awoke in the morgue after being dead for approximately 28 minutes. He had encounters with 13 angels and saw what he called a crystal city. He gave 117 prophecies from this NDE of which about 100 have come to pass in one form or another. Before his NDE he had been a violent bully that had caused harm to many in his life. He had been in his own words a "jerk" before his NDE but afterwards was committed to living a life of love and service. He now works as a hospice volunteer. He exemplifies the born again or new creation life taught in scripture.[37]

The Process of Salvation

For most of us, salvation is more of a process rather than a completely instantaneous event. We can begin to experience his love in seconds, you may have prayed to invite Jesus into your heart. But our transformation happens mostly over time. As a pastor I had once told me, we are saved from the 3 Ps. We are first saved from the penalty of sin, or the consequences. Next, we are saved from the power of sin. Lastly, we are saved from the presence of sin. Why all this sin talk though? Sin is missing the mark. It's breaking God's law. Since God is love, his law reflects love, so sin is really anything contrary to love.

You could think of salvation as a line. The more you embrace

God's love the closer you move to the light, the more one you are with God. The more you embrace sin such as hatred, fear, selfishness, lust, and pride the further you are from the light and more darkness you're in. The more darkness you're in, the more separate you are from God. That's also heaven and hell in a nutshell, and you don't have to be dead physically to experience this, though the feelings are more intense on the other side because you don't have the distractions on earth.

The Gospel of Jesus Christ

What is the gospel? Often, the gospel is presented as a formula with a few doctrinal beliefs you need to accept in faith. Believe that Jesus died for your sins and rose again. That's certainly part of the gospel or good news, but the gospel is much more than that. The gospel is about love and anywhere you see it, you see the good news in action. Maybe that's why the first four books in the New Testament are called the Gospels, the whole story is good news as is the Bible.

We can spend a lifetime trying to learn and take in the full gospel of love. Sometimes we may still have an incomplete picture of the gospel, yet, our journey of salvation has still begun. Keep this in mind with NDEers, why they may not express a belief in some set dogmatic gospel formula and yet are clearly born of the Spirit. In due time, we will all have the full picture of the gospel, as Paul told us earlier "We see through a glass dimly lit". (I Corinthians 13:12)

Isn't the gospel about faith in Jesus and God's grace? Yes, but your faith which is to trust or embrace must be rooted in love or it will come to nothing. God's grace or unmerited favor is also rooted in love (John 3:16, and Roman 8?) The cross itself is rooted in love. Jesus felt all of our sins and sorrows leading up to the cross and at the cross. On the cross, a massive infusion of love was released that washed away sin, it's difficult to explain. As the scriptures say 'love covers a multitude of sins" (I Peter 4:8) Jesus was the friend who loved us enough to lay down his life for us.

Some may not fully know how Jesus plays in, but if one embraces love fully, they are embracing Jesus and everything that Jesus was about. One may not know the full extent of the gospel but love and cherish what you have been given and seek to have all that is available.

There actually were people in the New Testament that followed God but lacked a complete understanding of the gospel. One such man was Apollos. Acts 18:24-26 says

> 24 And a certain Jew named Apollos, born at Alexandria, an eloquent man, and mighty in the scriptures, came to Ephesus.
>
> 25 This man was instructed in the way of the Lord; and being fervent in the spirit, he spake and taught diligently the things of the Lord, knowing only the baptism of John.
> 26 And he began to speak boldly in the synagogue: whom when Aquila and Priscilla had heard, they took him unto them, and expounded unto him the way of God more perfectly.

Notice that he was greatly praised for his knowledge of and fervency for God. He doesn't sound like an "unsaved" man bound for "hell". Had he died, he would most likely have been welcomed into heaven. His knowledge, however, was made more complete when Aquila and Priscilla instructed him. The world today is probably filled with many Apollos who only have an incomplete knowledge but are nonetheless followers of God. They may not even fully embrace further truth at first because they cannot comprehend it yet. They may not be able to on this side of heaven.

A False Gospel

If the heart of the gospel is love, can there be such a thing as a false gospel? The answer is yes. Paul references one in Galatians which was about salvation by works. The issue of works goes to placing people under bondage. Instead of having love which is what grace and faith are all about as your center, you are distracted by something else. This does take away from Christ and his supreme act of love on the Cross. Anything that takes you away from such love can become a false gospel to you. It's not faith and works, but a faith that works.

Universal Aspect of Salvation

Universal Salvation in the NDE

One criticism of the Near-Death Experience is that salvation seems to be nearly universal. Virtually everyone goes to heaven. I've read conflicting reports that place the number of people that have hellish NDEs as high as 12.5% and as low as 1%. I'm not sure how they calculate it. Often an NDE that starts off hellish will turn more heavenly and peaceful when Christ or God rescues the person. There are some NDEs where the entire experience is hellish. Only about 18% of those that die and come back remember having an NDE. The other 82% might have had an experience but cannot recall it. One reason might be that if they had a hellish one, it was so traumatic that they blocked it out. It could also be true that the experience was so wonderful that they could not bare to come back to this world. We don't know. The real number of hellish NDEs could be higher if the other 82% could remember. Plus, some NDEers may be afraid to come forward for fear of embarrassment or shame having had a negative NDE. Others may simply not want to talk about it because it was too painful.

Without speculating and simply going off what we do know, the minority of NDEers seem to go to hell. Many NDEers one might expect to have a hellish NDE actually had a positive one. So there does seem to be universal salvation of humanity. Can this be squared with the scriptures? I believe the answer is an overwhelming yes.

Universalism is not necessarily absolute

When I say there is a universal aspect to salvation I'm not speaking of universalism in an absolute sense. I subscribed to absolute universalism for about 10 years which meant that I believed every person would be saved no question about it. I came to reject this view for a less extreme one. The main issue I began to see was with blasphemy of the Holy Spirit which is the complete and knowing rejection of Jesus and his way. This is way more than simply unbelief or doubt, you know the truth and completely reject it.

The Pharisees had accused Jesus of healing by the power of Satan and this is where Jesus teaches on Blasphemy of the Holy Spirit. (See Matthew 12:31,32; Mark 3:28, 29; and Luke 12:10) They saw the power of the Holy Spirit in Christ working miracles but rejected him in the face of such undeniable truth. The situations in Hebrews chapters 6 and 10 are also probably referring to the blasphemy of the Holy Spirit which is talking about a sin from which you cannot return.

Jesus did say this was the only sin that would not be forgiven in Mathew 12:31, 32

> [31] "Therefore I say to you, every sin and blasphemy will be forgiven men, but the blasphemy *against* the Spirit will not be forgiven men. [32] Anyone who speaks a word against the Son of Man, it will be forgiven him; but whoever speaks against the Holy Spirit, it will not be forgiven him, either in this age or in the *age* to come.

Blasphemy of the Holy Spirit is set up as an exceptional sin that is unforgivable. The general rule is that all other sins are forgiven. If this is the case, then the general rule should be that most people will eventually be saved. The scriptures never say specifically that anyone has or will ever commit this sin, not even Judas, so it's still hypothetically possible that everyone could be saved. Even if some do commit the sin, it would probably only be a tiny minority of the human race, otherwise, the exception would swallow the rule. There are passages that would back up this idea.

The fact that someone might commit Blasphemy of the Holy Spirit and not be saved doesn't bother me in that it preserves free will. To insist on an absolute universalism would be to deny free will, you're going to be saved like it or not. I'm hopeful that salvation might be universal, but it has to be at least theoretically possible to reject the Light and His Love.

Scriptures that teach Salvation as the General Rule

The Bible teaches that salvation is for the entire human race as a whole. The Bible is replete with such verses. I have only sought to give a few key scriptures which could be a much longer discussion.

The scriptures teach the restitution of all things such as in Colossians 1:20 "[20] and by Him to reconcile all things to Himself, by Him, whether things on earth or things in heaven, having made peace through the blood of His cross." This idea is taught is numerous passages (see Acts 3:21; II Corinthians 5:16-20; Ephesians 1:10)

The Bible also teaches that Jesus is the savior of all men (see I Timothy 4:10), that in Adam all die but in Christ, all will be made alive (I Corinthians 15:22; Romans 5:18). Jesus died for all sins. (I John 2:2; Hebrews 2:9). God will have all men to be saved. (I Timothy 2:4)

What about Eternal Punishment?

There are a few passages in scripture that refer to eternal or everlasting punishment in one form or another. One of the most well known ones is Mathew 25:46 "And these will go away into everlasting punishment, but the righteous into eternal life." There are two points that can be made about passages like this. The first is that the punishment or correction (the Greek word kolasis translated punishment could be translated as either) could be of an eternal benefit to the person without needing to be endless in duration.

Take for example, you might have done something wrong as a child and your parents disciplined you in a way that caused you to change direction and never do that again. Maybe you stole something and had to repay what you stole as well as apologize. The correction given you benefited you for your entire life because you chose never to steal again. The same could be true for everlasting or eternal correction. You decide to change direction at some point in the darkness and begin to move toward the light.

A few verses before in Mathew 25:41 it says "Then He will also say to those on the left hand, 'Depart from Me, you cursed, into the everlasting fire". Notice it uses the word fire to describe the punishment. Unfortunately, many Christians over the centuries have interpreted this to mean a literal fire. If this were true, this would be an absolutely barbaric and cruel punishment to say the least. No, fire in scripture is often used to refer to purification.

In Mark 9:49 it says "For everyone will be seasoned with fire, and every sacrifice will be seasoned with salt. This would include Christians being seasoned with fire. No Bible scholar would hold that we as believers are going to be seasoned with literal fire. It's understood to mean that we will be purified. In Zechariah 13:9 it says "And I will put this third into the fire, and refine them as one refines silver, and test them as gold is tested. They will call upon my name, and I will answer them. I will say, 'They are my people'; and they will say, 'The Lord is my God.'" (ESV) The same idea is taught in many portions of scripture (I Peter 1:7; Isaiah 48:10; Malachi 3:3; and Proverbs 17:3) Peter says that we will endure fiery trials in I Peter 4:12 "Beloved, do not think it strange concerning the fiery trial which is to try you, as though some strange thing happened to you". Clearly, fire is figurative and applies to believers and nonbelievers alike. The question arises then, do you want to go through the refiner's fire now and turn to the Light of Christ, or do you need further lessons in the refiner's fire after this life? It's better to take the refining now than later.

The second point about this eternal or everlasting correction is the actual meaning of the word in Greek. The Greek word translated eternal or everlasting is aiōnios with the root word being aion or aeon. Aion means age and is an indeterminable amount of time. This is where the Latin word eon comes from, such as eons of time. It could potentially mean without end but doesn't necessarily have to mean that. So aionios could more literally be translated age-lasting or age-abiding.[38] Young's Literal Translation translates Mathew 25:46 as "And these shall go away to punishment age-during, but the righteous to life age-during."

If God is going to reconcile the human race, then for the vast majority or possibly even everyone, it couldn't mean endless. Why would it need to be endless? Once the correction causes the person to see the error of their ways and change direction, the correction has done its job. It may take a while for some stubborn people for sure though.

You could think of eternal punishment as a Judge giving a life sentence to someone. It doesn't mean that the person will spend the rest of their life in prison, only that they could potentially if they don't make a change. Most people that have a life sentence will someday be released.

Many NDEers have been rescued out of hell by God or Jesus, two that we have looked at were Howard Storm and Angie Fenimore. Angie actually was made aware that hell functions more like a purgatory during her NDE which further demonstrates this point.[39] This is consistent with what we see in scripture. Remember that we saw Jesus between his death on the cross and resurrection going and preaching the gospel to those in hell in I Peter 3:18-20. The scriptures also teach in Romans 10:13 "For "whoever calls on the name of the Lord shall be saved." Notice there are no qualifiers that you must call out in this life. You do have to call upon him from the heart as it says a few verses earlier (Romans 10:9,10) so you can't fake it just to get out of jail free so to speak.

Some may be thinking, the word for eternal life that we are promised in Christ is also aionios. Does this mean that our life in Christ might come to an end at some point too? No, because Jesus said that we would never die in him, John 11:26 states "And whoever lives and believes in Me shall never die." So the eternal life we are given is without end.

A Possible Scenario

Someone might be thinking at this point. "I like what you're saying, but I've always been taught that once a person dies there's no hope of salvation for them". I understand this perspective, it's one I came from myself. A hypothetical scenario may be of some help. Imagine a person who has lived completely separate from God, who had no interest in Christ or his ways. This person may have even lived a selfish and cruel life. Now, this person dies. The person is declared dead, with his or her heart having stopped and no brain waves detected. The sheet is placed over his or her face. He or she begins to descend into hell and lands in a place of utter darkness. The person is there for eons of time, what feels like millions of years. Then the person thinks to call out to God. A light comes down and rescues them out of this place and takes them into a place of great peace and joy. The person feels unconditional love in this place and is saved from his or her despair.

What was eons of time in the darkness for this person was actually only a few minutes on earth. The person was dead as far as doctors were concerned but the process of death had not fully set in before being saved by the Light. The silver cord was still hanging on by a thread.

This hypothetical situation is actually a great hope that the near-death experience helps to lay out for us. It may be possible to accept hope for a loved one that has died without rejecting what one may have been taught. In the moments just after the person's "passing", they may be given an opportunity to embrace the Light. Many near-death experiencers such as Dr. Eben Alexander experienced this. He was in a place of darkness for what felt like centuries and then was rescued out.[40] Time is a relative thing, so eons of time on the other side can be a few minutes on this side. NDEers have confirmed that time is completely different over there. As it says in II Peter 3:8 "But, beloved, do not forget this one thing, that with the Lord one day *is* as a thousand years, and a thousand years as one day." This scenario is what this book has been saying all along. Remember, spending a lifetime away from God will not have seemed worth it if you have to spend eons in darkness before being given a chance to come into the Light, nor will having to relive harm you've caused to others in your life review. It makes sense to get right with the Light now.

9. OBJECTION!

We're now going to look at some of the objections that Christians have raised over the years to the near-death experience. We will also discuss some newer, more positive explanations of what the near-death experience might be that have been put forward.

Objections raised to the NDE

The Being of Light is Satan

One objection that has been raised to the near-death experience is that it's a trick of Satan. This notion was a more popular one in the 1980s and 90s. I remember a book that was written arguing this idea. The basic verse pointed to is "And no wonder! For Satan himself transforms himself into an angel of light." (II Corinthians 11:14).

One test Jesus gave to know if something is from God or the enemy is that we would "know them by their fruits" (Mathew 7:16). Well, what fruits are that? Paul gives us the fruits of the Holy Spirit "But the fruit of the Spirit is love, joy, peace, longsuffering, kindness, goodness, faithfulness, 23 [a]gentleness, self-control. Against such there is no law" (Galatians 5:22,23).

A primary example of a false light from Satan appearing to be from God would be that of religious cults. One thing you may notice with some cults is that they can speak of love and even sometimes practice what's called "love bombing". When you start to look deeper though, the "love" they speak of is shallow and superficial. They also can't seem to hold it together well. This is especially true of the leadership within these groups. The love ends up being highly conditional and controlling. This is a prime example of how Satan masquerades as an angel of light.

Is the NDE anything like this pseudo-love? Absolutely not! The love affirmed by the near-death experience is unconditional and respects people's free will in every respect. The fruits of the Holy Spirit marks everything about the being of Light in the NDE, and the people come back reflecting these fruits in their own lives. It can be said easily, that the Light is the Spirit of God and not that of Satan.

Stephanie Arnold became more compassionate and empathetic after her NDE. She was able to relate to people's pain more easily and was forever changed.[41] Most NDEers feel more compassionate after their experience.

Another aspect of the fruits the scriptures speak of is to bring the fruits of repentance. "Therefore bear fruits worthy of repentance" ((Mathew 3:8). Repentance is to change direction. You turn from sin toward God. Since God is love and his law is rooted in love, sin is anything contrary to love. This is exactly what NDEers come back doing for life, they embrace love fully and reject everything contrary to it.

As we saw earlier, the NDE doesn't sugarcoat sin in the slightest. Yes, there's unconditional love and forgiveness, but people are radically confronted with how their actions affected others in their life review.

The NDE doesn't contradict the faith and in fact, many near-death experiencers come to faith as a result of the NDE. We covered 3 near-death experiencers who came out of atheism into faith as a result of their near-death experience.

Another argument that demonstrates the Being of Light is not Satan is that of children's NDEs which are strikingly similar to adults. I find it difficult to fathom that God would allow Satan the freedom to deceive children. Children are pure of heart and were revered by Jesus.

Many Christians believe in a doctrine called the age of accountability which says that children are innocent and are not accountable for their sins until they reach a certain age. What the age is, we don't know. We don't know if it's the same age for each child under this doctrine. God will protect these children who have not reached the age of accountability and if they die as a child, they will automatically go to heaven. If the age of accountability is true, then it should rule out Satan's ability to deceive them on the other side.

Finally, the near-death experiences between those that are Christians before their NDE and those that are not don't vary significantly. They tend to be consistent with one another. Both frequently encounter the Light who shows unconditional love to them, and they experience immense peace and joy. Much of the heavenly scenes are also quite similar. Both experience things of beauty such as gardens, rivers, trees, elaborate buildings, etc. Yes, some Christians will experience more overtly religious imagery, but even some non-believers have experienced similar imagery, such as seeing God's throne or seeing the pearly gates.

The Near-Death Experience is a Hallucination

This argument was commonly held by many within the secular world in the past and has been adopted by some Christians to discount the near-death experience. Most researchers have since rejected this idea. You can still find a few hard-core atheists that will make the argument. Unlike hallucinations which often jumble and distort reality, near-death experiencers encounter a hyper-reality. NDEs overwhelmingly are a very coherent experience with no signs of delusion. The experiencers tend to be very clear in exactly what they experience and it tends to stay vivid in their minds for decades. In fact, they tend to remember the experience more clearly than most other experiences they have on earth.

Experiences tend to be consistent among NDEers. They tend to fall within patterns and to be logical. If people see other loved ones on the other side, it's ones that have previously died and not people still alive generally.

Dr. Steven Taylor in his article "The Puzzle of the Near-Death Experiences" notes most of the above but also points out that the near-death experience tends to create a calm serene sensation that is not consistent with a hallucination. Dr. Taylor is still not convinced that this is evidence of an afterlife but finds the hallucination of a dying brain hypothesis to be unpersuasive.[42]

There's also evidence gained from the study of the near-death experience that in no way fits a hallucination. People come back with information that you simply could not get from a hallucination. People come back having experienced what could only be described as a miracle.

You die once and then you're judged

Some Christians have objected to the NDE because of the verse in Hebrews which says "And as it is appointed for men to die once, but after this the judgment" (Hebrews 9:27). I believe there are two possible explanations that might make this verse more clear.

We know from the scripture itself that there were people that died and then came back to life. One person was Lazarus who was raised from the dead by Jesus (John 11:1-44). There are several other resurrections from the dead recorded in scripture as well. Obviously, those that were raised from the dead lived only to eventually die again at a later date. The notable exception, of course, was when Jesus was resurrected from the dead.

There's also examples in the Bible of people who never died. Two notable persons mentioned are Enoch (Genesis 5:22-24) and Elijah (II Kings 2:11). These are all exceptional cases, and most of us are not going to be raised from the dead or be assumed into heaven without experiencing death. Nor are we likely to flat line and have a near-death experience ourselves. What the verse of scripture may be getting at is a general rule that the vast majority of people will die once then go to their judgment.

The verse of scripture may also be speaking of death in the permanent sense. You will die permanently at some point, you will not be coming back to this life, and then have a judgment. NDEers will die again at some point and will not return as they did previously. Some near-death experiencers have since died. Interestingly, many near-death experiencers were actually told that it was not their time, they had to go back.

More positive views of NDEs

Some Christians have started to take a more positive view of the near-death experience even if they don't necessarily fully embrace it. I've heard some say that the NDE might be a dream or vision. At least with these views, near-death experiences are not seen as something sinister or to be summarily dismissed.

God used both dreams and visions in the scriptures to speak to people, so it can at least be something God uses to bring a message or spiritual experience to someone. God spoke to Joseph in the Old Testament through a dream to tell him he would rule over his brothers and be greatly blessed (Genesis (37:1-44). Later, God gave Joseph the ability to discern dreams for people which allowed him to gain favor with Pharaoh and prepare the people for famine (Genesis 41).

Today, many people have had wonderful experiences in dreams that bear similarities to the near-death experience or can give hope or a warning. Dreams and visions spiritually may also be part of how God will minister to people in the last days as it says in Acts, "And it shall come to pass in the last days, says God, That I will pour out of My Spirit on all flesh; Your sons and your daughters shall prophesy, Your young men shall see visions, Your old men shall dream dreams." (Acts 2:17).

I personally have had what are called visitation dreams. This is where a loved one that has passed away comes to you in a dream. The first dream I had was about a month after my father passed away in 2010. The dream was extremely lucid and vivid. I knew I was in a dream and that my father had passed and yet, also knew he was there visiting me. It felt as real as when one is awake.

Towards the end of the dream, I asked him how heaven was with Jesus, he said: "It's wonderful!". Wow! It sent tingles throughout my body. I actually experienced him whispering it in my right ear.

Another visitation dream was from my maternal grandparents who came to be about a week before our son was born in early 2014. My grandfather passed in 1984 and my grandmother in 1988. I never had a dream about them since their passing prior to this dream. I really had not given much thought to them over the years either. The dream came out of the blue. Like the dream with Dad, it was vivid and I knew I was dreaming and in contact with my grandparents. So I understand the power spiritually that a dream can have.

Most NDEers, however, have said that their experience was way beyond a dream and felt more real than life on this earth. This life pales in comparison to what they experienced in their near-death experience. Some researchers have noted that at the time of the NDE, there should not have been any brain activity which would rule out being a dream.

Another approach is to view the NDE as a type of spiritual vision. This is popular with the noted apologist, William Lane Craig who sees death as an intermediate state prior to the resurrection of the body. In this, he sees the near-death experience as a vision of the afterlife. People can get a glimpse of the world to come and possibly see Jesus, angels, departed loved ones, etc. They can also see heavenly beauty and be given a high degree of love, peace, and joy. His view is closer to what most near-death experiencers feel that they had.[43] The Apostle John was given many visions of Christ and Heaven throughout the book of Revelations much of which is comparable to the near-death experience. Though I appreciate Craig's perspective, I don't think a vision fully explains the NDE. These people had clinically died or were close to death, and their soul was taken to another realm in most cases. They actually experienced being in another dimension, not just seeing and hearing things from another realm but also tasting, touching, and smelling things in some cases. The sensation was not of seeing something out there, but actually being there. Remember, during Paul's near-death experience, it says he was "caught up" to the third heaven. (See I Corinthians 12:2,3) Many NDEers have the feeling of being transported to heaven as Paul did.

What Dr. Craig may be referencing is what some call a deathbed vision just before they pass. Strikingly similar to the near-death experience but as far as we can tell, they have not left their body at that point. There's one experience in scripture that stands out as a deathbed vision but prior to leaving his body and ascending into heaven, that of Stephen in the book of Acts which we discussed earlier.

10. SCHOOL

One thing that needs to be addressed which may seem like a tangent but will make more sense as we go forward is, why did God seem so harsh in the scriptures and in the Old Testament specifically? This seems to be a common question. God seems so severe, even cruel in the Old Testament but then gets "nicer" in the New Testament. The answers you tend to get from most Bible teachers are inadequate and unsatisfying. Many Christians discussing the near-death experience would never touch this subject, and many people not coming from a faith based perspective who would discuss it would use it to criticize the Bible. But if the NDE acknowledges scripture as inspired, we can't afford to be so dismissive.

This chapter will parallel our previous chapter entitled `Objection!". In that chapter, we covered some objections that Christians had to the NDE. Now we will be dealing with difficulties some have with the Bible, including many who have an interest in the near-death experience.

When you look at why, for example, there were so many capital offenses in the law of Moses, even for offenses such as working on the Sabbath, or why God commanded that entire groups of people be wiped out by the Israelites, the question above seems fair. Teachers of scripture will point out the extreme wickedness of certain people like the Canaanites which were to be exterminated. That they needed to be taken out because they had become like a cancer on the land and if they were not eliminated, the cancer would spread. They point out that they often had centuries to repent but didn't. Ok, fair enough, but it's still a hard thing to swallow.

With the severity of the law, they point out that the Israelites were set apart for God and had to remain pure until the messiah came. With Jesus, the law would be fulfilled, and you could then experience greater mercy. That's great for us, but it's still difficult to understand why God had to be so extreme.

I do think there's truth in what the teachers have to say but more has to be explained. There's a much deeper level of truth that most of them miss. I do believe that the Bible is divinely inspired by God. The writers and others were having experiences with God and being taught of God. God was guiding this process and even guiding the recording of these experiences and lessons for future generations which includes us today.

God Meets People Where They Are

There's also the human aspect of the scriptures as well. The writers of the Bible are experiencing and writing the spiritual truth that they learned from a personal, cultural, and religious context. God is relating to them within this context and meeting them whether they are. Not only is the writer coming from within a specific context but so were the people around him which were his original audience.

God starts where the person is but is also gradually helping them and his audience to grow and expand in this understanding. We comprehend this in at least one context, progressive revelation. It's also true for a progressive expression of God with human beings.

God's School

You could think of this as a school for the people of God, but really, the entire human race. Many early church fathers as well as others such as Martin Luther understood this concept throughout church history. It's not even a completely foreign concept to scripture itself. Paul said in Galatians 3:24,25 "Wherefore the law was our schoolmaster, to bring us unto Christ, that we might be justified by faith. But after that faith has come, we are no longer under a schoolmaster" (KJV)

Is this to say that the law or history recorded in the Old Testament is of no value? No, we may not be in the Old Testament school, but we take the lessons we learned there with us. We still benefit from the lessons we learned in first grade, but we don't need to remain in first grade. We can learn from the truths of the Old Testament but not seek to emulate everything they did. I think this point is missed because there are groups that want to impose the Law of Moses on the church and in some cases, civil society today.

The Feedback Loop in the NDE

The near-death experience actually works much like this, the experience can be guided by our personal, religious, and cultural beliefs to some extent. God will start there and then begin to expand our understanding. He will give us the bigger picture. Mellen-Thomas Benedict in his NDE was told about the "feedback loop" that people sometimes get based on their beliefs when they cross over.[44] This is why one needs to study the NDE and scriptures collectively and not in isolation.

The NDE parallels the Bible because it comes from the same common source. It can help us to understand the Bible better in that the experience is placed within our own cultural context generally speaking. It's not in competition with the Bible but can be a tool in reading it, much like a Bible dictionary, concordance, commentary, etc, only this like the Bible is a record of actual encounters with God so it's more powerful. The NDE can bring the truths of the Bible alive to someone in a fresh new way.

Expanded Understanding in the Old Testament

You do start to see an expansion of understanding even in the Old Testament before you get to the New Testament. Take the story of Jonah, the prophet was told to go to Nineveh to tell the people to repent or judgment would follow. The prophet didn't want to go and wanted to see judgment fall on the Ninevites. God would not let Jonah go because he desperately wanted to spare the people from Judgment. Finally, after being swallowed in the belly of a whale and nearly dying (he may actually have died, we aren't sure), he went and preached to Nineveh, and they repented. Jonah was actually unhappy that they did, even to the point of being suicidal. Jonah acknowledged God's great mercy in Jonah 4:2 "Ah, Lord, was not this what I said when I was still in my country? Therefore I fled previously to Tarshish; for I know that You are a gracious and merciful God, slow to anger and abundant in lovingkindness, One who relents from doing harm." A few verses later God says in 4:11 "should I not pity Nineveh, that great city, in which are more than one hundred and twenty thousand persons who cannot discern between their right hand and their left-- and much livestock?" In this exchange, you start to see a greater picture of God's mercy and compassion for humans than you did earlier in the Old Testament when he summarily ordered the Canaanites to be wiped out, every man, woman, and child. It wasn't that God acquired greater mercy or compassion, it was that the people of God were not ready to see it yet.

We begin to see a more clear picture of God's desire as the Old Testament progresses with this verse in Hosea 6:6 "For I desire mercy[a] and not sacrifice, And the knowledge of God more than burnt offerings." God wants us to express mercy and grow in our knowledge and understanding of his ways and not simply rely on what we have always done or believed.

Humanities Harshness Being Reflected Back

So why was God so harsh in the Old Testament, or at least in the earlier portions of it? Because it was a reflection of humanity's own harshness at the time. You can see this when Jesus said this concerning why divorce in the law of Moses was so easy in Mathew 19:8 "He said to them, "Moses, because of the hardness of your hearts, permitted you to divorce your wives, but from the beginning it was not so." The law expressed the reality of where the people were at the time, but not God's ideal, and God was not going to leave them there.

Jesus Accelerates our Spiritual Growth

When Jesus came, he was going to grow the believers of God up more quickly and radically than they had in the past. This was going to be an accelerated course in love, forgiveness, compassion, mercy, and much more. He was going to be taking us rapidly to higher levels in our understanding. He did this in many ways that we can see in the gospels. In the Sermon on the Mt which is recorded in Matthew 5-7, he challenges us to go much further than we ever had.

He questions the standard of an eye for an eye in verses 38-44 and says to turn the other cheek and to pray for those that mistreat you. To go the extra mile with them. It's not that the eye for an eye standard was all bad, it presents a principle of equity in justice within the law of Moses. Now Jesus is calling us to something even higher than strict justice but to mercy. For mercy should triumph over judgment. (See James 2:13). That is the message of the cross itself, that we can gain mercy over what we really deserve.

Jesus called his followers in Matthew 5:44 to "love your enemies". The law of Moses had already introduced loving your neighbor as yourself. (Leviticus 19:18), but loving your enemy was a radical idea to the Jews at this time. This was going the next mile in their spiritual understanding.

Jesus also expanded the understanding of the law by internalizing aspects of it. To look at a woman in lust in your heart was adultery. To hate your brother in your heart was now murder within your heart. (See Mathew 5:21-30)

Jesus also began to teach a higher standard for crime and punishment within the Law of Moses. We get the story of the woman caught in the act of adultery in John 8:1-11. This exchange within those verses are especially pertinent:

4 They say unto him, Master, this woman was taken in adultery, in the very

act.

> 5 Now Moses in the law commanded us that such should be stoned: but what sayest thou?
>
> 6 This they said, tempting him, that they might have to accuse him. But Jesus stooped down, and with his finger wrote on the ground, as though he heard them not.
>
> 7 So when they continued asking him, he lifted up himself, and said unto them, He that is without sin among you, let him first cast a stone at her. (John 8:4-7)

Notice that Jesus doesn't in any way criticize the law of Moses. He accepts that adultery is a sin and worthy of judgment. It would be just for her to be punished for this sin. What he introduces to the discussion is having greater mercy. Since we have all sinned, we should not sit in judgment of others, though, we all deserve judgment. He doesn't directly attack capital punishment but makes it functionally impossible if you're going to apply his love to the situation. Put the "he who is without sin, let him cast a stone at her" in our own context. "He who is without sin, let him inject the needle."

Once you embrace the higher principles of Jesus, you can't go back. As it says in Luke 9:62 "But Jesus said to him, "No one, having put his hand to the plow, and looking back, is fit for the kingdom of God." A person in college cannot go back to the first grade spiritually speaking, it's upward and onward in the kingdom of God.

Earth Is A Giant School

One thing about life is that we are all here to learn and grow, and earth is our school. This is true for us individually and collectively and our journey throughout history. What are the major lessons we are here to learn? The lessons revolve around love and anything related to love such as kindness, compassion, forgiveness, etc. This is really what this whole discussion has been about in this chapter. The Bible centers around Christ, of course, but the core of Christ is love. You see this in his life, death, resurrection, and teachings and its theme throughout scripture.

This idea of life as a school has been confirmed by many near-death experiencers. One example is that of Jean R. Jean was told that earth was a big school and a testing ground where you could learn hands-on through experiences. Some people come to learn just one or a few lessons and others come to learn many lessons. Some people come to make a global impact in their life, such as Martin Luther King, while others come to have a smaller more personal impact.[45] The goals set before coming to earth vary widely but tend to all connect to love in one form or another.

The Classrooms of Heaven

George Richie had a near-death experience while in the army during WWII, his NDE was triggered by an illness. George actually met with Jesus and had a life review. He was given a detailed tour of heaven. One thing that George saw in heaven was what looked like a huge university campus with many classrooms. He was able to enter some of these classrooms and witness advanced instruction going on.[46] So heaven itself is a school and has literal schools that people can attend. We thus don't automatically know everything when we get to heaven and our learning continues in the next world and for eternity.

11. EVIDENCE

The evidence for scripture and Christianity is substantial. Many have offered arguments for both over the centuries. The study of evidence for the faith is called apologetics. Apologetics comes from a Greek word apologia where we get our word apology from, but can also mean to offer a defense of something. The latter is what is intended with apologetics.

Evidence for the near-death experience is also beginning to mount. So much so that many scientists are starting to study the subject and take it more seriously. There have been a few books written directly dealing with evidence for the NDE but such evidence is usually covered in an overall discussion of the topic.

What this chapter will attempt to do is offer evidence for both scripture and the near-death experience that blend and complement one another. The evidence presented here will parallel with each other and help to form a case for scripture and the NDE. As I've said before, the NDE can be used to form a new type of apologetic that until recently has never been considered. The Bible can also help to substantiate near-death experiences. What is exciting to consider, is that if there's evidence for the supernatural today in NDEs, then why could there not have been supernatural events going on during the times of scripture? The inverse question is also valid, if supernatural events such as miracles happened in scripture, why couldn't they be occurring today? The truth for both can be a revolving door.

Clear Testimony

When we look at scripture and the near-death experience, we start off with a clear testimony of the text and experience. With the Bible, we have three lines of evidence that help to establish that it is a reliable document. The first line is that the scriptures are supported by numerous manuscripts that are close in time to when the original books were authored. This is true, especially when speaking of the New Testament. There are 25,000 complete or partial manuscripts of the New Testament, some dating within a few decades of when the book was originally penned. There's 36,000 direct quotations of the New Testament from the Early Church Fathers alone in addition to direct manuscripts. The sheer number and closeness in time of the manuscripts to the original writing dwarf any other writing in Antiquity. Nothing can compare to the New Testament documents, including those of Plato or Aristotle which have much fewer preserved copies and are much later in time than the originals. We can rest assured that what we are reading is the same as what the original writers wrote, including Paul, John, and Mathew.

The Bible is externally consistent and writes about historical places that still exist or have been shown to have existed in the past which is not always the case for other ancient texts whether secular or religious. The Bible has been substantiated by other historical documents as well as archeology. We know that certain people and events actually existed or happened. This includes the existence of King David, the city of Jericho, and Pilot's rule.

The final line for the reliability of scriptures is that it's internally consistent throughout. Though the Bible was written by over 40 authors; over 1,500 years, in 3 languages and continents, the theme of Christ is central throughout.[47] These pieces of evidence do not directly prove the Bible to be divinely inspired or spiritually true, but it indirectly demonstrates that the text is reliable in its testimony. We're not dealing with fictional stories and fabrication. This indirectly can be said to show that God has guided and preserved the record of scripture and is a good starting point to further discuss its validity.[48]

The NDE like scripture starts with a consistent testimony of itself. The near-death experience has been shown through extensive research to be a highly lucid experience that appears to be more real and clear to experiencers than their waking experiences on earth. This in spite of the fact that such experiencers are clinically dead or unconscious at the time of the experience. The experience is well organized, logical, and consistent in nature. The experience also tends to be a fairly universal event with similarities across cultural lines. All of which doesn't prove that it is a spiritual event by itself but helps to demonstrate that it's a real event.[49]

Seeing the Impossible

What if you could see things in a room with total clarity while being unconscious or clinically dead? What if everything you observed was later verified by people who were fully conscious in the room with you? What if your vantage point was from the ceiling looking down? For me, this would be strong evidence for a non material reality. This is exactly what so many NDEers have claimed to see while flatlined which was later confirmed by medical staff and other persons present in the room. There is no good scientific explanation for this that has ever been presented. Many doctors, nurses, and scientists have been baffled by such confirmed accounts.

One such case that was well documented was Pam Reynolds who was medically brought to a near-death experience as possible to do experimental surgery. Her body was cooled and she had no brain or heart activity in 1991 while in surgery. She claims that she popped out of her body and was floating above the operating table and observed everything that was occurring in vivid detail. She could see and hear every instrument used and could see everything that the doctors and nurses were doing. She could hear everything being said. Everything she observed and heard was later confirmed to be accurate by medical staff present in the room.

This stunned her doctor who stated that medically it would

be impossible for her to see or hear anything. Besides her medical state, her eyes and ears were completely covered. Pam went on to have a more extensive NDE where she saw the Light, met past relatives, and got to ask questions.[50]

What if a person could be completely unconscious or clinically dead and could not only see what was occurring in the room but was able to move beyond the room and see things occurring in other locations? Possibly in other parts of the hospital or even other locations miles, even hundreds or thousands of miles away? Wouldn't this even be more amazing evidence of a spiritual reality? Even fully conscious people cannot see things occurring in other locations with their natural senses generally speaking. They certainly can't see things occurring miles away as if they were there. This too is exactly what some NDEers have experienced.

One highly documented case of a person being able to see beyond her room in the hospital while having a NDE was a woman named Maria. Maria came out of her body and was able to see a blue tennis shoe on a third floor ledge. She was able to describe the shoe and its positioning in great detail. She told her social worker who went to the location described and was able to confirm every detail of the account given by Maria.[51]

George Richie had a detailed near-death experience in 1943 while serving in the military during World War II. His NDE was triggered by an illness during basic training. In one part of his experience, he traveled miles away to a location in Jackson, Mississippi where he saw the sign for an all-white nightclub. He had never been to this city and knew nothing about this nightclub. The sign and nightclub were later confirmed exactly as George had recounted in his story.[52] One side note to this story, George had grown up in the South in Virginia in the 1920s and 30s and held many racist views commonly held at the time. After his experience, he noted that his racial prejudices were gone which speaks to the transformational power of the NDE.

George and Maria saw events from a distance that they couldn't have otherwise seen in the natural which is similar to an event that some experience while conscious called remote viewing. The difference being that George and Maria appear to have been conscious outside their body and unconscious within their body. Jesus appeared to have had a remote viewing recorded in scripture. John 1:48 "Nathanael said to Him, "How do You know me?" Jesus answered and said to him, "Before Philip called you, when you were under the fig tree, I saw you." We aren't told how far away the fig tree was from Nathanael who he saw, but judging from his reaction, it wasn't close and wasn't something Jesus could have seen with his natural field of vision. Nathanael responded in verse 49 by saying "Nathanael answered and said to Him, "Rabbi, You are the Son of God! You are the King of Israel!"

Seeing Those Unknown

What is amazing is that most people that NDEers see during a near-death experience are people that have previously passed away. People that have had NDEs almost never see people on the other side that are still alive. If the experience was a hallucination one would expect that you would see those still alive as well as possibly those that have passed. More astonishing than this is when NDEers see people such as relatives that they didn't know on earth or even know of their existence.

Colton Burpo was only three years old when he had his near-death experience. While on the other side, he met his sister who had died in utero due to a miscarriage. His parents had never told Colton of this miscarriage. There are many NDEs where people, especially children, who see a sibling they didn't know they had on the other side. Some died in the womb while others died as babies or young children. The existence of the sibling is later confirmed to them by other family members.

Colton also met his great-grandfather who he never knew on earth and had not been told anything about. His Papa had been especially close to Colton's father when he was a boy. Colton came back speaking of Papa which stunned his parents as did his meeting his sister. Colton was able to identify his great-grandfather when shown an old family album.[53]

If the NDE was just a product of a dying brain seeking to ease the dying process for the person, why and how would it come up with people that the person never knew of or about on earth? This is one of the strongest pieces of evidence for the near-death experience being a genuine spiritual event in my opinion. This along with people being able to see things in other locations that they could not normally see offers compelling evidence that we do have a soul which survives physical death.

The scriptures also have an account where Jesus was able to give information to a woman that in the natural he could not have otherwise known. I'm speaking of his encounter with the woman at the well. He was able to tell her that she had been married five times and was living with a man she was not currently married to. This convinced the woman that Jesus was, in fact, the Christ. (See Mathew John 4:1-26)

Fulfilled Prophecies

The nature of most prophecies whether in scripture or the NDE as it relates to global events tends to be veiled until they're clearly fulfilled. Then we look back and it's obvious to us. Apocalyptic prophecies may be veiled because they have the potential to be changed, that they are not written in stone. You see this with the near-death experience but you also see this with scripture. God would send the prophet out with a dire warning of what will happen if change does not occur. Often the people didn't heed but in a few they do.

For most global prophecy in the NDE, it tends to parallel what you would find in scripture such as the book of Revelation. Things such as wars, famines, and economic collapse are common in both. There are also predictions of a time of great peace and love where the world experiences a spiritual revolution which also mirrors the scriptures when it speaks of the millennium or new earth. This is the case for NDEers whether they were Christian and knowledgeable about Bible prophecies or not. Until the prophecies come to pass, however, they are open to interpretation which is true for both scripture and the near-death experience.. What really provides strong evidence for the spiritual truth of both the Bible and the NDE is the clearly fulfilled prophecies that we have. I'm thinking of such prophecies such as Christ in his first coming and prophecies that have come to pass within the NDE.

There are over 300 fulfilled prophecies of Jesus coming that were predicted in the Old Testament. The odds of these prophecies being fulfilled by mere chance are astronomically small. To fulfill just 8 by chance would be less than one in one billion. So to fulfill 300 leaves virtually zero chance that it could have happened randomly with just one person. Some prophecies are things well out of Jesus' control as a human such as where he would be born.

Just a few of these fulfilled prophecies include the fact that he would be born in Bethlehem. (Micah 5:2 fulfilled in Matthew 2:16). He would be a great prophet like Moses (Deuteronomy 15:18 fulfilled in John 7:40-42). Jesus would have a triumphant entry into Jerusalem before he was to be killed (Zachariah 9:9 fulfilled in Luke 19:35-37). That Jesus would die by crucifixion (Psalm 22:14-16 fulfilled in Mathew 27:31, Mark 15:20, and John 19:15,16). The prophecies of his death by crucifixion were made centuries before the method of execution was devised by the Romans. These prophecies help to prove that the Bible is divinely inspired and that Jesus was, in fact, the Christ, the perfect Son of God.[54]

One astonishing NDEer to look at in terms of fulfilled prophecies was Dannion Brinkley. It is estimated that he made 117 prophecies from his NDE in 1975 and 100 of them have already come to pass. He predicted that a former actor with the initials

RR would become President of the United States which happened with Ronald Reagan. He predicted a major nuclear explosion would occur that would kill thousands of people which would be connected to wormwood. This occurred in 1986 with Chernybol. Interestingly, Chernybol in Russian means wormwood and refers to the dark green plants that grow around the area. The Bible itself may also have predicted this event in Revelation 8:10,11 which says "Then the third angel sounded: And a great star fell from heaven, burning like a torch, and it fell on a third of the rivers and on the springs of water. The name of the star is Wormwood. A third of the waters became wormwood, and many men died from the water, because it was made bitter." Dannion also predicted the first Gulf War and the collapse of the Soviet Union.[55]

Resurrection from the Dead

Coming back from the dead would be the ultimate miracle that science could not explain and would give the strongest proof of a spiritual reality beyond this physical world. The resurrection of Jesus is the most attested to miracle in history and has led countless numbers to faith in Christ over the last two thousand years. There are resurrections within the near-death experience, though none would be as profound as Jesus because he came back never to die again. In a sense, all NDEs are resurrections but many came back due or partially due to medical intervention. It may still be amazing that they were able to return, possibly still a miracle in itself. The ones we want to focus on, however, were ones where the person did not return due to medical intervention and were completely left for dead.

The Resurrection of Jesus

The Disciples that were with Christ all saw him after his resurrection. This is attested to in several places within the New Testament. The women that went to the tomb saw him as well. (See Mark 16, John 20, and John 21) Later, Paul records that he saw the risen Christ as did over 500 people in I Corinthians 15:3-6. These were eyewitnesses to the resurrection and many were still alive when Paul wrote this. We examined Paul's own encounter with Jesus on the road to Damascus and how it profoundly changed his life.

In Acts 1:3 "to whom He also presented Himself alive after His suffering by many infallible proofs, being seen by them during forty days and speaking of the things pertaining to the kingdom of God. " These proofs were enough that the Apostles were willing to suffer persecution and death for the sake of Christ. Paul and all of the Apostles except for John were martyred for the faith, having suffered things such as beatings before being eventually killed. The authorities did attempt to kill John but were unable to do so and eventually exiled him to the Aisle of Patmos. (see Revelations 1:9-11)

No evidence from history exists that would refute the testimony of the Apostles concerning the risen Christ. Rome and Jewish officials would have had ample reason to wish to refute such a claim by the Apostles but were unable to do so.

The Jewish leaders attempted to claim that the disciples stole the body which is recorded in scripture. (see Mathew 28:13) This was to possibly save the life of the Roman soldiers who faced a death sentence if they fell asleep on duty or deserted their post. It was also a poor attempt at damage control. The Jewish leaders spread the rumor but lacked any evidence to substantiate it. In fact, it would be unlikely that the body was stolen because armed Roman soldiers were posted; the tomb was also protected by a large stone blocking the entrance; and it was also sealed by Rome. The stone may have weighed as much as a ton. To break a Roman seal was a capital offense. In the event that the disciples did steal the body, they would have died for a lie and would have been fully aware that it was a lie. Such character by the disciples would have violated everything we knew of them in terms of their ethics and message.

Some have argued that Jesus didn't actually die but revived

and left the tomb to meet with his disciples. This itself would be a miracle in that Rome took care to ensure that he was dead before even taking him off the cross. (see John 19:31-36). He would have to free himself from the burial garments that he was wrapped in from head to toe.(see John 19:39, 40 and John 20:6, 7), Jesus would then have to get through the posted guards, a heavy stone, and a seal to get to the disciples. Taking everything into account, the resurrection seems more plausible to say the least.[56]

Resurrections from a Near-Death Experience

Emmanuel Tuwagirairmana who we discussed earlier, had a profound resurrection experience with his NDE. At the end of Emmanuel's near-death experience, he was told that he would be going back to earth which didn't please him. Jesus touched him and he was revived in his body. The body was full of maggots and had begun rotting by this point. His companions, who had taken refuge within the school, began to see his body moving and were amazed. He had been dead for seven days and had revived without any medical assistance.

A doctor in Australia was given a vision of Emmanuel and told to go help him with his arm. The doctor got on a plane and went to give medical aid to Emmanuel. The doctor was told exactly where to go and what to bring to find and assist Emmanuel. The doctor was able to save his arm. Much of Emmanuel's arm had been eaten away but was told by Christ to refuse surgery to remove it and wait on him when he was finally taken to the hospital.

In Emmanuel's story, one sees a reflection of the Bible in the events and miracles that surround it. He was resurrected from the dead after being dead for 7 days! This is a miracle on the order of Lazarus' resurrection in scripture. (See John 11:1-44) Both men were raised by Jesus. One thing to think about, if a man in modern times can experience such a miracle and it's attested to by living people today, then it should give us further hope when we read miracles in the Bible that they in fact happened as well.

The doctor's vision of being able to know where to go and help Emmanuel is much like the vision that Peter was given to go witness to Cornelius in Acts 10:1-48. Again we see the parallel of scripture with the event surrounding an NDE of Jesus working in both to perform His will and to show forth his power.

After Emmanuel returned he began to minister and share his NDE to help lead people to Christ. Everywhere he ministers, there are reports of miracles that follow him. Much like the Apostles had in the book of Acts. In one report, a local witch known for her powers suddenly lost them when she came in contact with him. In another report, Emmanuel was imprisoned for sharing the gospel and he prayed. A wind came in and destroyed the prison! He was promptly released.[57] This is much like Peter's miraculous release from Prison in Acts 12:1-19.

Remember George Rodonaia, he had been assassinated by the KGB in the former Soviet Union in 1976. He was rushed to the hospital where he was worked on but eventually was pronounced dead. He laid in the morgue for 3 days and came back to life with no medical assistance as they were performing an autopsy on his body. This shocked many doctors and nurses and led about 15 people to come to Christ as a result. It's interesting that he was dead for 3 days and then rose again, which is how long Jesus was in the grave before his own resurrection. George did, however, pass away permanently in 2004, whereas Jesus ascended into heaven never to die again.[58]

Dannion Brinkley was dead for 28 minutes with the sheet being placed over his head and had been moved to the morgue when he came back to life. Dannion came back profoundly transformed and with many visions of the future that came to pass.[59]

Miracles from the Near-Death Experience and Scripture

There are so many miracles recorded in scripture and the New Testament specifically that volumes could be written about them. The same is true for the near-death experience. It would probably be better to simply mention a couple that are profound and not overwhelm you.

Spontaneous Healings

Mellen-Thomas Benedict who we have mentioned earlier was actually on hospice with terminal brain cancer when he had his NDE. He was not expected to live more than a few months. So even if he had died and revived, the process of slipping into clinical death briefly should not have made any difference in his ultimate prognosis. Yet, when he came back to life, his brain cancer was completely gone. His doctor, not willing to call it a miracle, simply referred to it as a "spontaneous remission". Mellen went on to live another 35 years until his permanent death in 2017.[60] Much like Mellen, George fully recovered from his life-threatening injuries when he woke up in the morgue and would go on to live another 28 years. In George's case, it did stun his doctors who recognized it for what it was, a miracle.

We read of literally dozens of miracles that Jesus and his disciples performed in the gospels and the book of Acts. This includes raising people from the dead as he did with Lazarus (John 11:38-44). As well as raising a widow's son from the dead. (Luke 7:11-17) When scripture says in Matthew 9:35 "Then Jesus went about all the cities and villages, teaching in their synagogues, preaching the gospel of the kingdom, and healing every sickness and every disease [i]among the people.", that about sums it up. One has to believe that some of those miracles were terminal illnesses such as advanced stage cancers like Mellen or life-threatening injuries like George. George and Mellen were both healed by the Light of God just like those healed by Jesus during his earthly ministry.

Enhanced Hearing and Restored Eyesight

Ken Ebert had a serious biking accident at the age of 18 in 1984 which caused him to briefly die. He saw his body lying on the pavement and then was in darkness. He was eventually taken to the Light and a peaceful garden. He was met by a being of light that took a female form who he conversed with. He was asked if he wanted to return or not, and Ken chose to return. When Ken returned, he noticed a greater sensitivity to light and electricity. Things like light bulbs would blow out and other electrical devices would cease to work. He noticed watches that he would wear would stop working quickly after he bought them. It was strange that he bought 3 watches, and they all stopped working at the same time of the day. The first watch started working again once the second one stopped.

The most amazing change with Ken was in his hearing. He could now hear conversation way in the distance, even in a whisper, especially if it concerned him. He was able to distinguish specific conservations. His hearing didn't get louder but was more acute and pinpointed. Distant conversations were always heard in his left ear. Ken's enhanced hearing was almost like a new superpower that he acquired and not just a sense of better hearing. His improved hearing seems to have a spiritual quality to it.

We know that Jesus healed the deaf and gave them back their hearing in many places within the gospels. He healed a deaf and mute man in Mark 7:31-37. In a sense though, Jesus may have had his own spiritual enhanced hearing in that he would know the thoughts of other people. As it says in Luke 5:22 "But when Jesus perceived their thoughts, He answered and said to them, "Why are you reasoning in your hearts?" Might he have heard the thoughts in his mind? Quite possibly.

Robert Bare was a former LAPD police officer years earlier working in the riot squad. He was a rough man who had engaged in many beatings and assaults over the years in his job. Robert had his near-death experience in 2009 on a plane when he suffered a massive heart attack which caused him to die for 45 minutes in spite of doctors and paramedics who worked on him on the plane to revive him. He left his body twice and eventually went through a tunnel and was taken into the light. He experienced a dramatic life review that forever changed him when he came back. He went into nonprofit work helping unpriveleged children. One part of his NDE that stood out to him and would be relevant to his physical changes when he returned was the beautiful colors that he saw in the Light. Some colors that don't even exist on earth.

When Robert returned to earth, he had a sensitivity to electrical things much like Ken. For Robert, it was with microwaves and fireplaces. Microwaves would go out and fireplaces would suddenly turn on. The most amazing change though was in Robert's eyesight. Over a six month period from returning from the Light, his vision began to dramatically improve. He went from seeing 20/90 to 20/10 which is actually better than perfect vision! This, of course, is an amazing miracle in that his visual change can be measurably verified.

Like Ken though, there appears to be a spiritual quality to Robert's improved vision. At times, he is able to see images of the past, present, and future all at the same time. We know that Jesus had a spiritual dimension to his vision as well, being able to see Nathanael under the fig tree as we have already discussed.

We know that one of Jesus's favorite types of healing recorded in scripture was when he would heal the blind and restore their sight. Several passages could be listed of Jesus healing the blind. One passage of interest is a blind man who was mentioned by name. "Blind Bartimaeus" was healed by Jesus as he and his disciples were entering the city of Jericho. Bartimaeus was a beggar in the city who apparently had a reputation that followed him since he was known by name. Bartimaeus requested that he be given his sight and Jesus simply said that his faith had made him well without even laying hands on him. His sight was immediately given to him. He had been blind from birth so he had no familiarity with sight before his miracle. (See Mark 10:46-52)

It's interesting that this miracle took place in Jericho because the city was known for another famed miracle recorded in the Old Testament. (See Joshua 6:1-27) God told the prophet to have the people march around the city walls and when they did this, the walls came crumbling down by the power of God. This prophet's name was Joshua. Jesus' name is a Greek form of the Hebrew name Joshua! Funny how God works sometimes!

Artistic Giftings from the Light

There have been many artistic giftings that people have received from NDEs as well as STEs. The two that will be looked at are in music and artistic painting. The gifts of the Spirit are mentioned in I Corinthians 12-14 but the list there is not an exhaustive list. No doubt, God can and does give some people with artistic giftings that can come directly from an encounter with him.

Lyla's Musical Endowment

Lyla had a near-death experience decades earlier that would lead to her musical talents coming to the surface. Before her NDE she had no musical background and didn't know how to play any musical instrument. She was shown a new path for her life when she returned to earth during her experience that included her music. She, like many other NDEers, was not afraid to pursue this new path because she felt she had nothing to lose. She had already died. She quickly acquired the ability to play and compose when she returned and the music constantly comes to her.

Lyla performs and composes new age music which is strongly connected to the near-death experience due to it being so ambient and transcendental in nature. Many NDEers have reported hearing music that sounds much like new age music and some like Lyla have composed music in an attempt to capture what the music in heaven is like for the rest of us.[61] The music has a way of helping to transport us to that spiritual realm. This too is why this music is so wonderful for meditation. I personally love this music and use it in meditation and when I am working from time to time.

Remember, it was a host of Angels singing and bringing forth music when Jesus was born. (See Luke 2:13, 14) So from scripture, we know that music plays a part in heaven. Revelations 14:2,3 says

> And I heard a voice from heaven, like the voice of many waters, and like the voice of loud thunder. And I heard the sound of harpists playing their harps. ³ They sang as it were a new song before the throne, before the four living creatures, and the elders; and no one could learn that song except the hundred *and* forty-four thousand who were redeemed from the earth.

Akiane Kramarik's Ability from Christ

Akiane Kramarik's family was originally from Lithuania before moving to the United States. Her family were atheists and had not told her anything about God or Jesus when she had a profound visitation from Christ at the age of 4. She didn't have an NDE but an STE. Jesus gave her the ability to paint masterful pictures and told her to start drawing and painting which she started doing immediately and continues to this day over 20 years later. Her most famous painting of Christ was painted at the age of 8 years old called "Prince of Peace". The image of Jesus has been confirmed by many near-death experiencers as the one that they saw during their NDE. This includes Colton Burpo. Akiane has spoken all over the world and been interviewed on many shows including the Oprah Winfrey Show and Katie Couric Show.[62] This goes to show that God is still gifting people whether by a near-death experience or in their everyday life just as He did in scripture.

CONCLUSION

There is a strong correlation between the Bible and the near-death experience. The Bible contains near-death experiences as well as other spiritually transformative experiences. These experiences guided the lives of those in scripture and were critical to the spiritual formation of the Bible itself. Two key events that are at the core of the New Testament and Christian faith are the resurrection of Christ and conversion of the Apostle Paul. The resurrection is an extraordinary near-death experience in its own right. Paul was converted through an experience similar to an NDE and then later went on to have a near-death experience. Without Paul and the resurrection, you have no Christianity or New Testament. As Paul said "And if Christ is not risen, then our preaching is empty and your faith is also empty." (I Corinthians 15:14)

At the same time, the near-death experience has confirmed the validity of the Bible. Both by direct confirmation of its inspiration as well as by confirming the core teachings of scripture such as the centrality of love. The NDE also confirms that heaven is real and that we do have hope for life in the next world. God is Light both in terms of the light we see but also, He is the spiritual light of this world.

Many near-death experiencers have encountered Jesus on the other side and some have come to faith in him as a result of the experience. Jesus is always who he is recorded to be in scripture, that is, the Son of God and savior of the world. Jesus heals physically, emotionally, and spiritually in both the scriptures as well as the NDE.

The near-death experience confirms that there is a judgment after this life, which many call the life review and that salvation is also real. Salvation not just from the darkness, but in the complete restoration to our creator.

The evidence for both the Bible and near-death experience parallel each other and both complement one other quite nicely.

The near--death experience is a modern phenomenon that both confirms and graphically illustrates what was recorded in scripture thousands of years ago. It helps to connect our world to that of the ancient world of the Bible. As it says in Hebrews 13:8 "Jesus Christ is the same yesterday, today, and forever." The NDE demonstrates this point for us. The near-death experience has the potential to become the strongest apologetic or argument for Christ to the modern world, so far removed from the times of scripture.

ABOUT THE AUTHOR

The author, Jay W. Spillers, practiced law for several years in Utah before moving to Montana. Jay currently lives in Montana with his wife Linda and their son Timothy. Jay is an avid writer and has been studying the near-death experience extensively for over 20 years. He wrote this book as a labor of love about a subject that is near and dear to his heart. If you would like to contact the author, you may email him at spillers72@gmail.com. You may also follow further spiritual discussions with Jay on Facebook at https://www.facebook.com/Spiritual-Discussion-Page-106913824248676/?modal=admin_todo_tour.

[1] Blue Letter Bible. "II Corinthians 12:4". "Strong's Concordance", 2019. https://www.blueletterbible.org/kjv/2co/12/2/t_conc_1090004

[2] Williams, Keven, "Emanuel Tuwagirairmana's Near-Death Experience" Near-Death Experiences and the Afterlife, 2017, https://www.near-death.com/religion/christianity/emanuel-tuwagirairmana.html

[3] Williams, Keven, "Howard Storm's Near-Death Experience", Near-Death Experiences and the Afterlife, 2016 https://www.near-death.com/experiences/exceptional/

howard-storm.html

[4] Dov Steinmetz, ""Revelation" on Mount Horeb as a Near-Death Experience" Journal of Near-Death Studies, Summer (1993): 199-203 p. ; 23 cm. , republished online UNT digital library, https://digital.library.unt.edu/ark:/67531/metadc798907/m2/1/high_res_d/vol11-no4-199.pdf

[5] Maksimonus. "BBC: PAM SEES GOD. NDE Pam Reynolds. Amazing! Full version!". Posted (April 2009). https://youtu.be/WNbdUEqDB-k

[6] Eadie, Betty. "Embraced by the Light", Gold Leaf Press, 1992

[7] Sunfellow, David "Dannion Brinkley", "NDE *Stories*", April 3, 2016, https://ndestories.org/dannion-brinkley/

[8] Sunfellow, David "Mellen-Thomas Benedict", "NDE *Stories*", , June 22, 2019, https://ndestories.org/mellen-thomas-benedict/

[9] Sunfellow, David "Angie Fenimore", "NDE *Stories*", January 5, 2019, https://ndestories.org/angie-fenimore/

[10] Kynmcintuff. "Howard Storm - Other Life in the Universe" Posted (May 2012) https://www.youtube.com/watch?v=wbKmPrlgIPU&t=42s

[11] Williams, Keven, "Howard Storm's Near-Death Experience", Near-Death Experiences and the Afterlife, 2016 https://www.near-death.com/experiences/exceptional/howard-storm.html

[12] HeavenVisit. "A Glimpse of Eternity - Ian McCormack" Posted (October 2011) https://youtu.be/ZO0O5PxFbeE

[13] Sunfellow, David "Dr. George Rodonaia", "NDE *Stories*", August 31, 2013, https://ndestories.org/dr-george-rodonaia/

[14] Sunfellow, David "Mellen-Thomas Benedict", "NDE *Stories*", , June 22, 2019, https://ndestories.org/mellen-thomas-benedict/

[15] NDE Accounts-Afterlife Stories. "Karen Thomas - NDE - Freewill" Posted (March 2017). https://youtu.be/WDqLqiIdcbA

[16] Sunfellow, David "Dannion Brinkley", "NDE *Stories*", April 3, 2016, https://ndestories.org/dannion-brinkley/

[17] Steven Wagner, "Near-Death Experiences: Glimpses of the Afterlife, First-Hand Accounts of Coming Back from the Great Be-

yond" Liveaboutdotcom (May 2019) https://www.liveabout.com/near-death-experiences-glimpses-afterlife-4076597

[18] Jenn, "New Age in the Old World: Plato's Account of a Near-Death Experience" *The Search for Life After Death* (November 2015), https://thesearchforlifeafterdeath.com/2015/11/09/new-age-in-the-old-world-platos-account-of-a-near-death-experience/

[19] New Life Covenant Church "What Heaven Is Like | Dean Braxton" Posted (October 2018). https://www.youtube.com/watch?v=S91jGFnHgCg

[20] Sunfellow, David "Nanci Danison", "NDE *Stories*", , June 21, 2013, https://ndestories.org/nanci-danison/

[21] "Are There Animals and Pets in the Afterlife?: Yes! According to Near Death Experiencers". Life After Death Experiences, Evidence of Life After Death", http://www.lifeafterdeathexperiences.org/are-there-animals-and-pets-in-the-afterlife-yes-according-to-near-death-experiencers/

[22] Steven Wagner, "Near-Death Experiences: Glimpses of the Afterlife, First-Hand Accounts of Coming Back from the Great Beyond"

[23] Williams, Keven, "Dr. Dianne Morrissey's Near-Death Experience", Near-Death Experiences and the Afterlife, 2016, https://www.near-death.com/experiences/exceptional/dianne-morrissey.html

[24] Sunfellow, David "Angie Fenimore", "NDE *Stories*", January 5, 2019, https://ndestories.org/angie-fenimore/

[25] Fellowship of the Inner Light. "Sharon Milliman - God's Unconditional Love" Posted (April 2019). https://www.youtube.com/watch?v=Kt5XAATzIMw

[26] NewHeaven NewEarth. "Near-Death Experiences: God Loves Everyone!" Posted (October 2018). https://www.youtube.com/watch?v=AzzFL3xMALg

[27] Maksimonus. "BBC: PAM SEES GOD. NDE Pam Reynolds. Amazing! Full version!". Posted (April 2009). https://youtu.be/

WNbdUEqDB-k
[28] Eadie, Betty. *Embraced by the Light*, Gold Leaf Press, 1992
[29] HeavenVisit. "A Glimpse of Eternity - Ian McCormack" Posted (October 2011) https://youtu.be/ZO0O5PxFbeE
[30] Long, Jeffrey. "Tricia B NDE", "NDEF",https://www.nderf.org/Experiences/1tricia_b_nde.html
[31] Life After Death Experiences, Evidence of Life After Death"https://www.medicalbag.com/home/specialties/neurology/near-death-experiences-more-real-than-real/
[32] Barker, Tricia "The Life Review", "Be the Light of Your own Healing", January 19, 2019 https://triciabarkernde.com/2017/10/31/the-life-review-in-a-nde/
[33] Neal, Mary, *To Heaven and Back; The True Story of a Doctor's Extraordinary Walk With God*, Circle 6 Publishing, 2011
[34] Sunfellow, David "Angie Fenimore", "NDE *Stories*", January 5, 2019, https://ndestories.org/angie-fenimore/
[35] HeavenVisit. "A Glimpse of Eternity - Ian McCormack" Posted (October 2011) https://youtu.be/ZO0O5PxFbeE
[36] Ring, Kenneth, *Lessons from the Light: What We Can Learn from the Near-Death Experience*, Moment Point Press Inc., September 2006.
[37] Sunfellow, David "Dannion Brinkley", "NDE *Stories*", April 3, 2016, https://ndestories.org/dannion-brinkley/
[38] Sulem, David. "God's Plan for All", CreateSpace Independent Publishing Platform, 2017, chapter 17, (Paperback and ebook) https://godsplanforall.com/
[39] Sunfellow, David "Angie Fenimore", "NDE *Stories*", January 5, 2019, https://ndestories.org/angie-fenimore/
[40] Sunfellow, David "Dr. Eben Alexander – NDE", "NDE *Stories*", November 4, 2019, https://ndestories.org/dr-eben-alexander/
[41] Arnold, Stephanie, "How a Near-Death Experience Changed My Life" SA, May 30, 2014, http://stephaniearnold.net/2014/05/30/how-a-near-death-experience-changed-my-life/
[42] Taylor, Steven, "The Puzzle of the Near-Death Experience, Just the Hallucinations of a Dying Brain or Something More Mysterious?" *Psychology Today* (2014), https://

www.psychologytoday.com/us/blog/out-the-darkness/201410/the-puzzle-near-death-experiences

[43] William Lane Craig, "What Happens When We Die?", Reasonable Faith with William Lane Craig, https://www.reasonablefaith.org/writings/popular-writings/practical-issues/what-happens-when-we-die/

[44] Sunfellow, David, "Mellen-Thomas Benedict NDE", "NDE Stories", June 22, 2019 https://ndestories.org/mellen-thomas-benedict/

[45] Long, Jeffery MD, "2932 Jean R. 6166", NDERF-Near-Death Experience Research Foundation, https://www.nderf.org/Experiences/1jean_r_nde_6166.html

[46] Richie, George. *Return from Tomorrow*, Revell, 1996.

[47] Smith, Brandon, and Whitebol, Jeremy, "The Truthfulness of the Bible", LifeWay, https://www.lifeway.com/en/special-emphasis/read-the-bible/articles/the-truthfulness-of-the-bible#fb

[48] Rhodes, Ron Dr., "Manuscript Evidence for the Bible's Reliability", Reasoning From the Scriptures Ministries, 2016, http://ronrhodes.org/articles/manuscript-evidence-for-the.html

[49] Long, Jeffrey MD., "The Nine Lines of Evidence", The New Dualism Archive, 2012, http://www.newdualism.org/nde-papers/Long/Long-_2012--1-2.pdf

[50] Maksimonus. "BBC: PAM SEES GOD. NDE Pam Reynolds. Amazing! Full version!". Posted (April 2009). https://youtu.be/WNbdUEqDB-k

[51] IANDS, "Key Facts about Near-Death Experiences", "International Association for Near Studies", August 29, 2017, https://www.iands.org/ndes/about-ndes/key-nde-facts21.html?start=2

[52] Richie, George. "Return from Tomorrow", Revell, 1996.

[53] Burpo, Todd, and Vincent, Lynn, *Heaven is for Real, A Little Boys Astounding Story of his trip to Heaven and Back*, Thomas Nelson, Nashville, TN 2010.

[54] Fairchild, Mary. "Old Testament Prophecies of Jesus", "Learn Religions", June 25, 2019, https://www.learnreligions.com/prophecies-of-jesus-fulfilled-700159

[55] Katy, "The Prophecies of Dannion Brinkley", "The Supernatural Zone", https://www.qsl.net/w5www/brinkley.html

[56] McDowell, Josh. "Is There Really Solid Evidence for the Resurrection of Jesus?", "Josh McDowell Ministries", 2001, https://www.bethinking.org/did-jesus-rise-from-the-dead/q-is-there-really-solid-evidence-for-the-resurrection-of-jesus

[57] Williams, Keven, "Emanuel Tuwagirairmana's Near-Death Experience" Near-Death Experiences and the Afterlife, 2017, https://www.near-death.com/religion/christianity/emanuel-tuwagirairmana.html

[58] Sunfellow, David "Dr. George Rodonaia", "NDE *Stories*", August 31, 2013, https://ndestories.org/dr-george-rodonaia/

[59] Sunfellow, David "Dannion Brinkley", "NDE *Stories*", April 3, 2016, https://ndestories.org/dannion-brinkley/

[60] Sunfellow, David "Mellen-Thomas Benedict", "NDE *Stories*", , June 22, 2019, https://ndestories.org/mellen-thomas-benedict/

[61] Diamond, Debra. *Life After Near Death; Miraculous Stories of Healing and Transformation In the Extraordinary Lives of People With New Found Powers*, Wayne, New Careers Press, Inc., 2016.

[62] Kramarik, Akiane. "Akiane Gallery", "Akiane Page", https://akiane.com/about/

Made in the USA
Monee, IL
23 December 2024